"Like most church kid: heroes to emulate, and the less heroic the heroes looked. They had seeds of greatness buried in the clay of sin. How could it grow? When would the harvest come? Why do we have these stories of men who seemed great, but instead were greatly broken? Pastor Stephen's meditations shine a clear light on King David's life. After you read this, you'll know yourself, David, and the Only True Hero more deeply. David's life offers us many lessons to live in this truth: there is only one pathway to genuine transformation."

> **Mike Wright**
> Pastor, Littleton Christian Church; Moderator, Evangelical Presbyterian Church Presbytery of the West
> Littleton, CO

"For two consecutive summers our church lived in the books of 1 and 2 Samuel as we preached through them each Sunday. They were rich sermons, but in many ways they were also jarring sermons, for both the one in the pulpit and those in the pews. We saw heroes with warts as big as their noses and a king whose relationship with God was a roller-coaster—faithful now unfaithful, rejoicing now crushed, wise now foolish. Yet behind these ups and downs, we also saw what God wants us to see: the constancy of his grace. I wish Stephen's book—with his relentless focus on the true Hero—were published sooner so I could have shared it with our congregation."

> **Benjamin Vrbicek**
> Teaching Pastor, Community Evangelical Free Church; Co-Author of *More People to Love*
> Harrisburg, PA

"Pastor Stephen loves the gracious gospel of Jesus, and he combines this love with a pastor's heart for seeing ordinary people take hold of this grace in their lives. Reading *Fierce Grace* is an opportunity to learn these loves from a brother and pastor who, like King David, has tasted and seen the goodness of the God of grace."

> **David Hoffelmeyer**
> Pastor, Trinity Presbyterian Church
> Sparta, IL

"Saints that daily deal with sin: the life of King David shows us the highs and lows of human leadership. We know him as a man of lust, adultery, and deceit, yet a man of great devotion and love for God. Taken from the life of David, *Fierce Grace* will be a strong and biblically trustworthy reminder that Jesus is the true hero of every story and the center of our daily walk. This is the kind of book that allows us to take an honest look at ourselves, our opportunities, and life struggles while encouraging us to see God's gospel as the sure foundation for every season."

Darren Casper
Executive Director, Plant Midwest
St. Louis, MO

"The church desperately needs to be bathed in God's favor drawn from all of Scripture. Read for a greater treasure of grace from God's story. Read for walking out the gospel every step of your journey. Read for sweeter and deeper fellowship with Jesus. Explore the fierceness of God's grace in 1 and 2 Samuel with Stephen."

Gabe Reed
Lead Pastor, Calvary Summitview Church
Denver, CO

"Pastor Stephen is spiritually mature beyond his years and is committed to the truth of the Word. His teaching brings clarity to Scripture and is applicable to everyday life."

Frank Wedel
Owner/Operator, Wedel Red Angus
Leoti, KS

BesorBooks

100% of the profits of this book will be donated to Covenant Theological Seminary for the training of future Church leaders.

Fierce Grace

30 Days With King David

Stephen R. Morefield

Fierce Grace
30 Days With King David

© 2018 Stephen Morefield
All rights reserved.

Stay up to date with Stephen's writing at facebook.com/besorbooks

Cover design: Ashley Foote
Interior design: Stephen Morefield with Benjamin Vrbicek
Author photograph: Doug Storie

Trade paperback ISBN: 978-1-7322755-0-8
Mobipocket ISBN: 978-1-7322755-1-5
ePub ISBN: 978-1-7322755-2-2

All emphases in Scripture quotations have been added by the author.

To Bobby, my Grandfather.
You called me to this long ago.
-Mighty

ACKNOWLEDGMENTS

2 Timothy 2:1

Thank you Morgan, my beautiful bride, for supporting and bearing with me throughout all that pastoring and writing requires. Your strength, honesty, and smile are gems that graciously keep me grounded and captivated.

I want to thank my fellow elders at Christ Covenant who not only allowed me to take on this project but who have gladly encouraged me from start to finish. It's a privilege to shepherd with you. Christ Covenant Church, this book comes from nearly a years' worth of sermons that we shared together early on. Thank you for being so kind and receptive to a young pastor then and now. It's good to be family.

I'm especially grateful for my team of editors: Rev. David Hoffelmeyer, Becky Miller, Rev. Michael Morefield, Kathy Mullen, Susan Wedel, and Rev. Mike Wright. Your insights were crucial. Special thanks to my editor in chief, Dad. I couldn't be more thankful for you and Mom, my examples in the faith.

Ashley, you did an incredible job with the cover and the Besor design work. Thank you for being a patient and kind sister! Doug, thanks for your photography. However, I was hoping you'd add in a little more hair. Benjamin, your expertise in publishing and interior book design was indispensable.

This book would have arrived half a year later, at best, without your insight. Thank you for sharing so much of your time to help a fellow pastor.

Finally, I'm thankful for the Jaeger family and their kind provision of the Wee Scottie Cabin for the writing of the rough draft. It was an incredible blessing.

CONTENTS

INTRODUCTION PART 1: WHY READ THIS BOOK **1**

INTRODUCTION PART 2: HOW TO READ THIS BOOK . . . **3**

PART I: RISE OF THE KING **5**

1.	That One Thing You Want *(1 Sam. 8)*	7
2.	More Than Meets the Eye *(1 Sam. 16)*	13
3.	The Hero We Need *(1 Sam. 17)*	19
4.	It's Complicated *(1 Sam. 18)*	25
5.	Security *(1 Sam. 20)*	31
6.	The Struggle *(1 Sam. 21:10–22:5)*	37
7.	Shortcut *(1 Sam. 24)*	43
8.	Identity Crisis *(1 Sam. 25)*	49
9.	The Muck and the Mire *(1 Sam. 27–28:2)*	55
10.	Delivered *(1 Sam. 29)*	61
11.	Search and Rescue *(1 Sam. 30)*	67
12.	Failure *(1 Sam. 31)*	73

PART II: REIGN OF THE KING **79**

13.	The Real Deal *(2 Sam. 2:1–11)*	81
14.	Everyone Has Faith *(2 Sam. 2:12–3:39)*	87
15.	Looking at the Heart *(2 Sam. 4)*	93
16.	Hope for the World *(2 Sam. 5)*	99

17. What's God Really Like? *(2 Sam. 6)*   105

18. The Covenant *(2 Sam. 7)*   111

19. History Matters *(2 Sam. 8)*   117

20. Are You Good Enough? *(2 Sam. 9)*   123

21. Assuming the Worst *(2 Sam. 10)*   129

22. The Fall of the King *(2 Sam. 11)*   135

23. The Restoration of the King *(2 Sam. 12)*   141

24. When Darkness Reigns *(2 Sam. 13)*   147

25. Weeping with Hope *(2 Sam. 15)*   153

26. God Wants Everything *(2 Sam. 18–19:8)*   159

27. Don't Fight Alone *(2 Sam. 21:15–22 & 23:8–39)*   165

28. How to Survive and Thrive *(2 Sam. 22)*   171

29. The Last Words of David *(2 Sam. 23:1–7)*   177

30. Wrath and Mercy *(2 Sam. 24)*   183

RECOMMENDED RESOURCES **189**

ABOUT THE AUTHOR **191**

NOTES **193**

WHY READ THIS BOOK

Why should you spend time learning about an ancient king from a far-away land? Fair question. Let me answer this in a few ways. First, history matters. We can't possibly understand our world if we don't study the past and apply it to our lives. David's life is real history that undeniably changed the world. But that's not the main reason you should read this book. Second, stories shape our hearts. There are things that we learn through stories that we can't possibly learn from user manuals or raw data. Stories have a unique way of connecting our heart to our mind, creating an effect on our whole person. David's story has no shortage of soul-shaping intrigue, characters, and plotlines. But this also isn't the main reason you should read this book.

In fact, the answer is rooted in something much bigger than David himself. And this is good news because, in the end, David and his flaws will disappoint you. He will also work as a mirror, revealing some of your brokenness too. Indeed, David matters most to us because his reign is one of the many previews that God has given his people of King Jesus. And this Jesus, the God-man, is the only one who will not disappoint.

1

He is also the physical descendant of David who is referred to as the second and greater David. Therefore, when David succeeds, we get a taste of Jesus' rule as king. When David fails, we're left with a hunger for the king we truly need. Every David story is truly a Jesus story. Indeed, the New Testament *assumes* that we are deeply acquainted with David when it speaks of Jesus. But maybe you're not convinced that Jesus matters all that much either. If that's the case, you'll actually be better able to assess your need (or lack of need) for Jesus after learning about the man who points to him. We need David's story more than we can imagine because we need Jesus. To find out why, I invite you to keep on reading.

HOW TO READ THIS BOOK

Here are four reading methods to consider as you start this book:

1. *Read This as a 30 Day Devotional:* Reading one chapter a day will make David's story come to life with all its interlocking adventures, relationships, and challenges. Fair warning though, this isn't a paragraph a day devotional. Each day brings you an entire story from Scripture, not just an isolated verse, followed by several pages that explain, illustrate, and apply the story to your life. Finally, you'll be given three questions to consider as you go about your day. If you're undecided on which method to try, I'd recommend taking the challenge and starting here.

2. *Read This Like Any Other Book:* Feel free to read this at your own pace, stopping and starting as you wish. Whether the book takes you a few days or a few months, there's no pressure to stick to a schedule. The whole

point of this book is to rest and feast upon the grace of God, not to check off boxes on a list.

3. *Use This as Curriculum for a Small Group or Bible Study:* Whether you've got a year-round weekly Bible study or a group that meets for a season, feel free to adapt this book to your needs and schedule. The three questions at the end of each chapter should provide leaders with good conversation starters.

4. *Use This as a Teaching or Preaching Aid:* Whether you're a pastor who's crunched for time or an overwhelmed lay leader, this study can help prepare you to teach on 1 and 2 Samuel. Each chapter comes with ready-to-use explanations of the text, at least one helpful illustration, and several applications you can use and adapt to your own setting.

Whatever method you choose, make sure to enjoy your time in God's Word. Be challenged yes, but rest in his grace. He's good. Very good.

PART I

RISE OF THE KING

Then all the elders of Israel gathered together and came to Samuel at Ramah and said to him, "Behold, you are old and your sons do not walk in your ways. Now appoint for us a king to judge us like all the nations"... And the LORD said to Samuel, "Obey the voice of the people in all that they say to you, for they have not rejected you, but they have rejected me from being king over them. According to all the deeds that they have done, from the day I brought them up out of Egypt even to this day, forsaking me and serving other gods, so they are also doing to you. Now then, obey their voice; only you shall solemnly warn them and show them the ways of the king who shall reign over them. So Samuel told all the words of the LORD to the people... He said, "These will be the ways of the king who will reign over you: he will take your sons and appoint them to his chariots... He will take your daughters to be perfumers and cooks and bakers... He will take the tenth of your grain and of your vineyards and give it to his officers and to his servants... and you shall be his slaves. And in that day you will cry out because of your king, whom you have chosen for yourselves, but the LORD will not answer you in that day." But the people refused to obey the voice of Samuel. And they said, "No! But there shall be a king over us, that we also may be like all the nations, and that our king may judge us and go out before us and fight our battles."

(1 Samuel 8:4–20)

THAT ONE THING YOU WANT

(1 Samuel 8)

Right now, in this moment, what is your deepest desire? Your answer matters more than you think. We base our lives upon our desires. You know the tug of desire if you've ever been in love, hit the snooze button, or felt your mouth water during a fast food commercial. Right, wrong, or complicated, our desires are powerful things. Unfortunately, our society fails to help us reign them in. We're told that we can do anything that satisfies us. But that's where we face a problem. What if my desires conflict with yours? Are all desires equal? Are all desires truly beneficial? Like the nation of Israel in 1 Samuel 8, we run headlong into the foundational truth that God alone reveals what is good and right.

The book of Proverbs puts it this way, "The fear of the LORD is the beginning of wisdom."[1] Everyone must come to terms with the fact that God alone has the right to determine truth. This, of course, includes the value of our desires. So how do we know which of our desires are good and which ones are dangerous? Even more difficult, how do we know when our good desires become distorted?

Dangerous Desires

Here's the situation: After calling a family to himself, God rescued them from slavery in Egypt, led them through the wilderness, gave them the promised land, and now has been guiding them with judges and prophets.[2] But there was a problem. The current prophet Samuel was old and his sons were in no condition to take charge after he died. God's people wanted something better. They wanted a king.

At first glance, this seems like a reasonable desire. Why not try a king? After all, everyone else had one. And here's where we begin to see the problem. Israel had a special job. Because of their unique relationship with God, they were called to be different from everyone else so that everyone else could see how good God was. But that's not what they wanted anymore. They wanted to be *"like all the nations"* (8:20). Samuel saw this as a personal rejection, but God saw to the root of this dangerous desire: *"they have not rejected you, but they have rejected me from being king over them. . . from the day I brought them up out of Egypt even to this day, forsaking me and serving other gods"* (8:7–8). Israel's desire to be like everyone else was a rejection of the God who had saved them.

In the past Israel had been forced to wait for God, trusting him when life grew difficult and dangerous. Now they wanted a shortcut, a king who could be seen, a man who could get things done. It all seemed so logical and clear. Who needs God when you've got that one thing you need?

Sadly, every desire that finds its fulfillment outside of God comes at a cost. And in this case, God asks Samuel to spell out the consequences for the people. Should they trust in a king, rather than God, the king will claim their sons, daughters, and servants for various kingdom work, he will take the best of their fields, vineyards, and cattle in taxes, and ultimately, he will take away their freedom. Simply put, the king will not lead like God has. He will take and take and take. That one thing we need always turns us into *"slaves"* (8:17).

Heavenly Hope

To be fair, not everything about the people's request for a king was bad. Despite our twisted motives, every person has a God-given longing for a hero. Far earlier in the Old Testament, the prophet Moses and the forefathers Jacob and Abraham spoke of a godly king who would come from the tribe of Judah to unite the people under God.[3] And so, even when Israel wrongfully rejects Samuel's warnings, we get a glimpse of these good, though skewed, longings for a hero: *"there shall be a king over us. . . that our king may judge us and go out before us and fight our battles"* (8:19–20). Do you see it? Even in their disobedience, the people long for someone who will lead, save, and judge them. We all share this longing. It's why we're tempted to hope in the next great politician, it's why we root for the clutch hitter in the ninth inning, and it's why we love movies where the good guy wins. We all long for a hero to make things right.

This longing goes deep because it's actually a longing for God himself. The Old Testament describes God as an eternal and mighty King: "The LORD reigns, he is robed in majesty. . . Your throne is established from of old; you are from everlasting. . . Mightier than the waves of the sea, the LORD on high is mighty!"[4] Likewise, the New Testament says that all of history is moving towards the day when God, from his heavenly throne, makes all things new, gives eternal life freely to his people, and crushes his enemies because he is the good King.[5]

From the first humans on, we've all longed for this king. So why does God let the people have a king? On the one hand, God is disciplining his people for trying to do life without him. On the other hand, God has eternally planned to use the office of king to point his people back to him. Providing Israel with a king is a fierce but good grace.

Have you ever looked for something in the wrong place? It's a daily occurrence in the Morefield house. Whether it's my keys, phone, or wallet, I'm always on the hunt. Predictably, I tend to look in several wrong places first before finding the right place, which, if I'm honest, is usually right in front of me.

Could the same be true of our desires? Are we looking in the wrong places? Could it be that those things we're searching far and wide for are actually longings meant to draw us closer to God? What would happen if we realized that our darkest desires were simply distorted longings for something good that only God himself could provide? Israel was seeking a king wrongly, but even in their sin, God, the true King, was graciously preparing something beautiful for them.

Pause for a Moment

Reflect: Think of one desire that separates you from God. How have you tried to justify this? What consequences have resulted?

Request: Trusting that our God is gracious to us even in our disobedience, ask him to show you the good roots of your distorted desire.

Respond: Instead of beating yourself up for every distorted desire you experience today, stop in that moment and thank God that he has purposely given you longings to draw you closer to Him. Say no to the distortion and ask Him instead to meet your needs.

The LORD said to Samuel, "How long will you grieve over Saul, since I have rejected him from being king over Israel? Fill your horn with oil, and go. I will send you to Jesse the Bethlehemite, for I have provided for myself a king among his sons"... And he consecrated Jesse and his sons and invited them to the sacrifice. When they came, he looked on Eliab and thought, "Surely the LORD's anointed is before him." But the LORD said to Samuel, "Do not look on his appearance or on the height of his stature, because I have rejected him. For the LORD sees not as man sees: man looks on the outward appearance, but the LORD looks on the heart"... And Jesse made seven of his sons pass before Samuel. And Samuel said to Jesse, "The LORD has not chosen these." Then Samuel said to Jesse, "Are all your sons here?" And he said, "There remains yet the youngest, but behold, he is keeping the sheep"... And he sent and brought him in... And the LORD said, "Arise, anoint him, for this is he." Then Samuel took the horn of oil and anointed him in the midst of his brothers. And the Spirit of the LORD rushed upon David from that day forward. And Samuel rose up and went to Ramah. Now the Spirit of the LORD departed from Saul, and a harmful spirit from the LORD tormented him... And David came to Saul and entered his service. And Saul loved him greatly, and he became his armor-bearer... And whenever the harmful spirit from God was upon Saul, David took the lyre and played it with his hand. So Saul was refreshed and was well, and the harmful spirit departed from him.

(1 Samuel 16:1–23)

2

MORE THAN MEETS THE EYE

(1 Samuel 16)

During World War Two the Allied forces realized that they needed to capture the island of Sicily before attacking mainland Italy. Unfortunately, the Axis powers knew this as well. "Everyone but a bloody fool would know that it's Sicily (next),"[1] said Winston Churchill. Facing this conundrum, two British officials came up with a genius plan: Operation Mincemeat. They would take a dead body, dress it up in a British uniform, attach a fake invasion plan, and then let the body wash ashore in German-occupied territory. Would it work? Would the Germans take the bait and move their troops out of the way or would they see right through it?

In this life, we often see so little. We're unable to pull back the curtain and understand tragedy, suffering, and frustration. Unlike God, we can't see what's really going on. And so we live in doubt and fear, coming up with our own solutions to problems that we can't fix. And that's why we have to learn to embrace God's sight. King David learned this truth and passed it on to his own children," The LORD. . . understands every plan and thought. . . serve Him with your whole heart and a willing mind."[2] So how do we learn to trust God's sight over our own?

Receiving Hope

God's people were at a critical juncture. They asked for a King, and God gave them King Saul. He was exactly what they had hoped for: impressive, mighty, and proud. But that was also the problem. He served himself, used God, and was leading Israel away from their faith.[3] The prophet Samuel was grieving. The people needed to move forward but how? Thankfully, God had a plan: *"The LORD said to Samuel, "How long will you grieve over Saul, since I have rejected him from being king over Israel? Fill your horn with oil, and go. I will send you to Jesse the Bethlehemite, for I have provided for myself a king among his sons"* (16:1). Notice who provides the hope. It's not Samuel, the people, nor King Saul. This time God says *"I have provided for myself"* a new king. This shouldn't be surprising. God is always in control and is always working to accomplish his good plans. God provides hope.

Receiving Wisdom

What's so special about the son of Jesse? Why will he be the new king? Samuel didn't know. When he arrived at Jesse's farm he lined up the boys and tried to figure out which one God wanted to become King. He had a hunch: *"When [the boys] came, he looked on Eliab and thought, 'Surely the LORD's anointed is before [me]' "* (16:6). Eliab was the oldest and surely the tallest, strongest, and best looking. Kind of like Saul 2.0. But God was looking for something different: *"the LORD said to Samuel, "Do not look on his appearance or on the height of his stature, because I have rejected him. For the LORD sees not as man sees; man looks on the outward appearance, but the LORD looks on the heart"* (16:7). God wasn't measuring by human standards. Samuel is forced to keep moving down the line. Once all the brothers have been passed over, Samuel was at a loss and asked Jesse: *"Are all your sons here?"* (16:11). Jesse had one more son but he was so insignificant that he hadn't been invited. Jesse speaks of him like he's a technicality. Sure, there's one more, but he doesn't really count. He's basically the runt. But this is the one God wants. God's wisdom is always different, and better, than man's.

Receiving Grace

Once David finally arrives from the fields God confirms that this is the one. And then something remarkable happens: *"Samuel took the horn of oil and anointed [David] in the midst of his brothers. And the Spirit of the LORD rushed upon David from that day forward"* (16:13). By anointing him, Samuel sets David apart for special work and by filling him with the Holy Spirit, God gives David what is needed to do the job. Think about God's grace here. What has David done to deserve any of this? Nothing really. God's choosing, calling, and equipping are all the result of grace. Without this, David would end up no different than Saul.

Ironically, just as God's blessing comes upon David, his judgment falls upon King Saul, and he becomes a troubled man. Even though Saul had rejected God and brought this upon himself, God is still gracious to him. David apparently was known for his musical skills and, in an irony of ironies, the rejected King hires the future King to come and minister to his troubled heart through music. Even Saul receives grace.

David doesn't rejoice in the suffering of this wicked king. Instead he ministers to him, serves him, and brings relief to his aching heart. We never receive grace for our sole benefit. Grace received must become grace shared.

There's one more thing we've got to see in this passage. David is anointed in this passage and the word for "anointed one" in Hebrew is *Messiah*. We make an enormous mistake if we read about David's life and think the main point is for us to be like him. Write this down: we're not David. We're not the *Messiah*. We're the people of God and we, like the people of God in David's day, are called to rejoice that God has finally given us a king, a messiah, a savior.

Like David, our King, Jesus, the Son of God, was overlooked by all but God the Father. He came from the same family and same little farm town as David and didn't have an impressive appearance or resume. But like David he brought grace to the suffering even though they didn't deserve it. And when God commenced the greatest rescue plan in history, the great enemy Satan couldn't help himself. Like Hitler who took the bait in Operation Mincemeat and suffered a great defeat, Satan took the bait and rejoiced in Jesus' death on the cross. He couldn't see what God could see or what God was doing. He couldn't see that this messiah was defeating sin, death, and evil forever. He couldn't see that this plan was in the works way back in 1 Samuel 16 when God chose David, the runt of a little farming family in a small town and the forefather of Jesus. We can't see what God sees. But thankfully we have a Savior who can.

Pause for a Moment

Reflect: Where else in the Bible does God use the weak, the unexpected, or even broken to complete his plans? Do some looking.

Request: How much of our lives are guided by the outward appearance of things? Ask God to give you his heart for what really matters.

Respond: Next time you're asked to help someone, make sure that you do it in a way that doesn't make you look like a hero. We're not David, and we're certainly not Jesus. Serve someone today in a way that helps them see the real hero.

And there came out from the camp of the Philistines a champion named Goliath of Gath... He stood and shouted to the ranks of Israel, "Choose a man for yourselves, and let him come down to me. If he is able to fight with me and kill me, then we will be your servants. But if I prevail against him and kill him, then you shall be our servants..." When Saul and all Israel heard these words... they were dismayed and greatly afraid... And David said to Saul, "... Your servant will go and fight with this Philistine." And Saul said... "You are not able to go against this Philistine..." But David said... "Your servant used to keep sheep for his father. And when there came a lion, or a bear, and took a lamb from the flock, I went after him and struck him and delivered it out of his mouth...The Lord who delivered me from the paw of the lion... will deliver me from the hand of this Philistine"... And when the Philistine looked and saw David, he disdained him... Then David said... "You come to me with a sword... but I come to you in the name of the Lord of hosts, the God of the armies of Israel, whom you have defied. This day the Lord will deliver you into my hand... that all the earth may know that there is a God in Israel, and that... the Lord saves not with sword and spear. For the battle is the Lord's, and he will give you into our hand"...And David... took out a stone and slung it and struck the Philistine on his forehead. The stone sank into his forehead, and he fell on his face to the ground...When the Philistines saw that their champion was dead, they fled.

(1 Samuel 17:4–51)

3

THE HERO WE NEED

(1 Samuel 17)

Every summer, millions of Americans flock to theaters to catch the latest superhero flick. How about you? Are you a Batman, Wonder Woman, or Hulk fan? [1] I have a complicated relationship with these movies. Sometimes I find them unrealistic and cheesy. At other times I find them intriguing, especially when they feature the sort of hero that I can't be.

We all need heroes who are greater than us. A mother can sacrifice everything for her children, but she can't control their choices forever. A husband can love his wife unconditionally, but he can't cure her cancer. Employees can work their hardest, but they can't control the next round of layoffs any more than a farmer can control the weather. At many points in life, every one of us reaches our limit and needs help. And that's why 1 Samuel calls us to trust the hero God provided. So who's that? Throughout the Bible, God sent many imperfect people, including King David, to point us towards the only real Hero who will rescue us all out of the darkness. [2] What does David teach us about this ultimate Hero?

A Hero That Sees

As the story begins, Saul has led Israel into battle against their fierce neighbors, the Philistines. Unfortunately, the Philistines have a not-so-secret weapon, the giant Goliath. All of Israel is terrified. Into this panic arrives David, still a young man keeping sheep for his father and playing music for King Saul. After dropping off supplies for his soldier brothers, David notices Goliath and begins asking questions. When David's oldest brother Eliab overhears the conversations, he grows angry, assuming that David is being nosy and morbid, sticking around to see the inevitable slaughter. Eliab is a realist, and he assumes Goliath will defeat Israel. It's a logical assumption, but it's godless.[3]

David, God's hero, sees something different. David's first words reveal this: *"For who is this uncircumcised Philistine, that he should defy the armies of the living God?"* (17:26). Unlike his brother, he doesn't see a giant: rather he sees a mere man insulting the living God. As one pastor notes: "God was the reality with which David (lived); giants didn't figure largely in David's understanding of the world, the *real* world."[4] David saw what God saw. Unfortunately, we tend to see things more like Eliab and the rest of God's people. Our sight is jaded and shaded by sin, fear, and lack of perspective. Just like the people of God, we need a hero who can see what we can't.

A Hero Who Represents

In modern times we have a hard time relating to Israel's fear of Goliath. How could one warrior make such a difference? Ancient warfare was up close and personal. Nations would select champions to represent the whole army in a one-on-one, winner-takes-all fight. Goliath was the representative for Philistia, and it was ultimately Saul's responsibility[5] to go out and represent Israel. But he didn't. Saul could see that he was no match for Goliath so he cowered in his tent.

At this point, David insists on serving as Israel's representative. Here's why he thinks he can: *"Your servant used to keep sheep for his father. And when there came a lion, or a bear, and took a lamb from the flock, I went after him and struck him and delivered it out of his mouth... Your servant has struck down both lions and bears and this uncircumcised Philistine shall be like one of them..."* (17:34–37). David knows that God provided him with the ability to care for his sheep in the past and in the same way, God will provide him with the ability to protect his people now. Whether in the wilderness or the valley, David can protect those under his care not because he is strong but because the strong God has called him to do so.

A Hero Who Wins

Goliath's bravado seems fairly well placed. We're told that he's nearly ten-foot tall, covered in over a hundred pounds of armor, and bears a spear made out of industrial equipment with a deadly fifteen-pound tip (17:4–7). Six times in the passage we're told that he mocks God and His people. Clearly he's confident. How could he possibly lose? David knows: *"This day the LORD will deliver you into my hand... That all this assembly may know that the LORD saves not with the sword and spear. For the battle is the LORD's, and he will give you into our hand"* (17:46–47). The battle is actually pretty anti-climactic. David slings a stone, brings down the giant,

21

and cuts off his head. It's fitting, because there's really no competition when God fights a man. Israel's representative has won, and the Philistines are routed as they flee.

Sadly, this is the part of the David and Goliath story where far too often you're told to now go out and fight the Goliaths in your life by faith, knowing that you will win. That's rubbish. That's not at all the point of the story.[6] And it's incredibly unhelpful. You can't beat your Goliaths. Israel couldn't beat Goliath. They needed their hero representative to rescue them with his God-given sight and power. The point of this story is that God does for us what we cannot do for ourselves. That's grace.

Let's be honest, hard work and a positive attitude will undoubtedly solve some of your problems. Nevertheless, there will come, if they haven't already, challenges that no amount of personal effort can solve. You, like Israel, will need a hero. You've always needed one. Thankfully, Jesus Christ is that hero. Like David and better than David, Jesus sees what is real, he represents you to the degree that your fate is completely tied to his own, and he always wins. Yes, he won by weakness, by dying on the cross, but he did it because God's weakness on the cross, or in a boy with a sling, is always greater than anything this world, sin, or the enemy can throw at us. You need a hero, and by grace you have one.

Pause for a Moment

Reflect: In the past, have you read the Bible as a story about heroes who we're supposed to imitate? What's the problem with doing this?

Request: As you read Scripture, ask God to show you how every story points us to Jesus and how we need him to do what we cannot.

Respond: List out some of the biggest problems or challenges in your life and some of the ways that you've tried to fix them. Now, list out the ways that Jesus promises to help you do what you cannot do, even if the promises are for the next life or require waiting.

The soul of Jonathan was knit to the soul of David, and Jonathan loved him as his own soul... Then Jonathan made a covenant with David...[and] stripped himself of the robe that was on him and gave it to David... David went out and was successful wherever Saul sent him... As they were coming home... the women... sang... "Saul has struck down his thousands, and David his ten thousands." And Saul was very angry, and this saying displeased him. He said, "what more can he have but the kingdom?" The next day... Saul... raved within his house while David was playing the lyre... And Saul hurled the spear, for he thought, "I will pin David to the wall." But David evaded him... Then Saul said to David, "Here is my elder daughter Merab. I will give her to you for a wife. Only be valiant for me and fight the Lord's battles." For Saul thought, "Let not my hand be against him, but let the hand of the Philistines be against him"... But at the time when Merab... should have been given to David, she was given to Adriel the Meholathite... Now Saul's daughter Michal loved David. And they told Saul, and the thing pleased him. Saul thought, "Let me give her to him, that she may be a snare for him..." Then Saul said..."The king desires no bride-price except a hundred foreskins of the Philistines..." Now Saul thought to make David fall by the hand of the Philistines. And when his servants told David these words, it pleased David... David arose and went... and killed two hundred of the Philistines... And Saul gave him his daughter Michal for a wife. But when Saul saw and knew that the Lord was with David, and that Michal... Loved him, Saul was even more afraid of David. So Saul was David's enemy continually.

(1 Samuel 18:1–29)

IT'S COMPLICATED

(1 Samuel 18)

It was a stunning spring day in the Harz Mountains of Germany. There was a pleasant breeze as Ben and Annie began their honeymoon with a hike. Suddenly, the clouds grew dark, rain began to fall, and the sky crackled. Ducking for cover they heard a zap. It was too late. Annie had been struck by lightning. Somehow Ben kept her breathing until a doctor could be found. Annie would live but would never walk again. A dream of a day had turned into a nightmare.

Life is complicated. So much good and yet so much bad. It's the woman who lands her dream job but then is left to raise her kids alone. It's the teenager who does great in school but struggles with an eating disorder. It's the grandparents who rejoice in their grandchildren who know Jesus and yet weep over the ones that don't. Life is complicated for everyone. Is there any consolation? 1 Samuel 18 tells us that there is. In the midst of it all, God is with us. Three times in this passage the people of God are reminded that God is with their hero David (18:12, 14, & 28) and each time they are reminded that as their representative, this means that God is with them as well. The same is true for Christians today, the Father is with Jesus, and this means that he is with us always as well.[1] So how do we remember this truth in both the good and bad of life?

Crediting God in The Good

There are ten verses in this passage that reference David's military success after defeating Goliath. Why was he so successful? The answer was simple: "*the LORD was with him*" (18:4) This doesn't mean David didn't plan, train, and fight hard, but rather that behind it all, God's hand was guiding him. God also provided David with support. David received the love of his nation, the love of Saul's daughter Michal whom he married, and the devotion of Saul's son Jonathan. The most surprising of these is the last.

After David defeated Goliath it would have been natural for Jonathan to see David as a rival. After all, how could Jonathan, the natural heir to the throne, compete with the Giant-killer? Surprisingly, something else happens: "*Jonathan loved him as his own soul. . . Jonathan made a covenant with David. . . And stripped himself of the robe that was on him and gave it to David*" (18:1 & 3–4). God gave David a friend who loved David as much as he loved himself. A friend who proved his devotion by making a covenant, or promise before God, with David that was clearly in David's best interest and not his own. And to seal the deal Jonathan gave David a gift, his royal clothes and equipment. Only God can provide a friend like this.

How are we reminding ourselves of God's good provision? It must be more than an "I wanna thank God" mention as a celebrity wins an award. Crediting God for our good must be a heart-level, moment-by-moment, desire to thank God for every good gift, success, and relationship we experience. God has provided it all.

Trusting God in The Bad

Despite all of God's good blessings, David's life was far from perfect. As he returned from defeating Goliath a new country song was composed by the crowds.[2] It went like this: "*Saul has struck down his thousands, and David his ten thousands*" (18:7). Saul was furious. Unlike his son Jonathan, he was unable to celebrate David. This hatred predictably erupts into violence as Saul hurls a spear at David. David escapes, but Saul was a clever man and knew that there was more than one way to kill a man.

Saul began to plot David's demise. "*Saul said to David, 'Here is my elder daughter Merab. I will give her to you for a wife. Only be valiant for me and fight the LORD's battles.' For Saul thought, 'Let not my hand be against him, but let the hands of the Philistines be against him*" (18:17). David is unaware of Saul's sinister secret, but God keeps him safe. Having no intention of making David his son-in-law, Saul revokes the offer and moves on to Plan B. He offers his younger daughter to David assigning him the quest of killing 100 Philistines. Saul was simply hoping that the law of averages would finally strike.[3] Saul was disappointed. David brought back twice the required number of dead enemies. The harder Saul tries, the more David is protected: Even in dangers that David is unaware of, God proves trustworthy.[4]

After Annie was paralyzed by the honeymoon storm, Ben brought her home to the United States knowing that life would never be the same. For the rest of their lives, Annie would never leave home, and Ben would only travel once. But

Ben trusted that the Lord was with them and would care for them. The situation forced him to keep life simple. He would teach class, serve his wife, and then study and write while she slept. And God was at work. Ben, who taught theology, ended up with the greatest writing output of any theologian in his day, becoming the strongest voice in the battle to defend the authority of Scripture within the Church. You see, Ben was Benjamin Breckenridge Warfield, and God was with him in both the good and the bad.

David, unlike Ben, was rescued from disaster in this passage. But he won't always be. This is just the start of his troubles. However, from the very beginning, in good and ill, God will prove to David that he is there.

The same thing will be true for David's later and greater descendant Jesus. God's power will be displayed in the goodness of miracles, ministry, and teaching. But God's power will also be displayed in the bad, protecting Jesus until it was his time to suffer. However, unlike David, God would abandon Jesus. He would leave him alone on the cross to cry out "My God, my God, why have you forsaken me?"[5] The Father would leave Jesus, accepting his death as payment for the forgiveness of sins, so that he'd never have to leave sinful David[6] or us for a moment. God's good presence in our lives, in the midst of the good and bad, is not dependent on us but on him who has died for us. And that is really good news.

Pause for a Moment

Reflect: Where are you right now? Are you experiencing good times, difficult times, or something in between? Whatever season you are in, is it drawing you closer to God or pushing you away?

Request: Praise the Father for abandoning Jesus on the cross so that he'd never abandon you, no matter what you are experiencing.

Respond: Next time a conversation about God comes up, make sure you talk about God's goodness to you during difficult times.

David said to Jonathan, "Behold, tomorrow is the new moon, and I should not fail to sit at table with the king. But let me go. . . If your father misses me. . . then say, 'David earnestly asked leave'. . . If he says, 'Good!' it will be well. . . but if he is angry, then know that harm is determined. . . Therefore deal kindly with your servant, for you have brought your servant into a covenant of the LORD with you"And Jonathan said. . .

"The LORD. . . Be witness! When I have sounded out my father. . . shall I not. . . disclose it to you. . . May the LORD be with you, as he has been with my father. If I am still alive, show me the steadfast love of the LORD, that I may not die; and do not cut off your steadfast love from my house forever, when the LORD cuts off every one of the enemies of David. . ." And Jonathan made a covenant with the house of David. . . on the second day. . . David's place was empty. And Saul said. . . "Why has not the son of Jesse come. . .?" Jonathan answered. . . Then Saul's anger was kindled. . . and he said. . . "You son of a perverse, rebellious woman, do I not know that you have chosen the son of Jesse to your own shame. . . For as long as the son of Jesse lives. . . neither you nor your kingdom shall be established. Therefore send and bring him to me, for he shall surely die." Then Jonathan answered. . . "Why should he be put to death? What has he done?" But Saul hurled his spear at him. . . In the morning Jonathan went. . . to the appointment with David. . . And they kissed one another and wept. . . Then Jonathan said. . . "Go in peace, because we have sworn both of us in the name of the LORD, saying, 'The LORD shall be between me and you, and between my offspring and your offspring, forever.' "

(1 Samuel 20:5–42)

SECURITY

(1 Samuel 20)

Who doesn't want to feel safe and cared for? When security is missing, we struggle. Soldiers often struggle with PTSD after lacking physical security for long periods of time. Those who lack relationships or live in abusive ones crave emotional and relational security. When the stock market takes a turn for the worse many fret over financial security. In all its forms, we desire security. David did. And as Jonathan supports his weary friend, we see something deeper at work than just friendship, we see a covenant.

A covenant is the most serious of promises, usually involving two parties, requiring certain responses. The history of the Bible is the history of God's people failing to keep up their end of the covenant with God. Thankfully, Christians know that Jesus died because of this, securing a covenant in which He keeps both ends of the promise. Indeed, God has made an absolutely secure covenant with us. How will it change our life if we live in light of this security?

Stability

David is living under constant fire: *"There's just a step be-tween me and death"* (20:3). King Saul is after his life and David is on the run. Where can David turn? There's only one person who has promised David security, his friend Jonathan. Even though returning to Jonathan means returning to Saul's realm, David knows that there is safety in their covenant re-lationship. And this safety opens the door for honesty and hard questions between the friends. Through their conversa-tion, David is able to make a plan. David will skip out on several public meals and Jonathan will gauge Saul's reaction to see if it's safe for David to come home. Their covenant provides the stability needed for David to continue on.

Where do you run when things fall apart? Do you have a covenant relationship to cling to? We all want to say we run to God, but do we really? What about the less obvious things we take refuge in, like zoning out in front of the TV, gossiping, eating or drinking more than we should, working too much, or doing "Christian" things to stay busy. These simply won't work long term. We can't just say that God is our source of security. We must go to him. We must sit before him. We must ask hard questions and wrestle with difficult answers. David's covenant with Jonathan points us to this greater covenant of security that we have with Christ.

Faithfulness

The stability we find in our covenant with Christ is not cheap. Jonathan chose to remain faithful to David, and it was costly. *"Saul's anger was kindled against Jonathan, and he said to him, '. . . as long as the son of Jesse lives on the earth, neither you nor your kingdom shall be established'* " (20:30–31). Keeping covenant with David meant losing his relationship with his father now and losing "his" throne in the future. There's always a price to be paid for this kind of faithfulness.

Dave Hartsock had gone on nearly 1,000 skydives in his life before something went wrong, a twisted chute. Instantly his mind shifted to the student strapped to him, the fifty-four-year-old grandmother, Shirley, who was on her first jump. As they fell, Dave reflected upon his life. They were 100 feet above the ground, and Dave knew there was only one way for his student to survive. He pulled the canopy open and inverted them before they hit the ground with a thud. Today, Shirley is perfectly healthy. Dave is a quadriplegic. "I did what. . . was necessary for taking care of my student," he said. "The most important thing [was] making sure Shirley got down safely. [I knew the risks, and I thought] OK, I can live with that."[1] Dave chose faithfulness and pain over faithlessness and ease.

This is no different than the cost Jonathan is willing to pay in being faithful to David through their covenant. As one scholar has said, "Life does not consist in achieving your goals but in fulfilling your promises."[2] Amazingly, David also makes a promise to be faithful to Jonathan and his family no matter what the future holds. This is God's love, steadfast love, and it is faithful no matter the cost.

Peace

In time, it becomes clear that Saul is bent on killing David. Jonathan sends David word, and they embrace before parting for good. *"They kissed one another and wept with one another. . . Then Jonathan said to David, 'Go in peace, because we have sworn both of us in the name of the LORD, saying, "The LORD shall be between me and you, and between my offspring and your offspring, forever"* (20:41–42). Can you see the result of their covenant? Peace. There's a horizontal peace between David and Jonathan and their families. There's a vertical peace with God because he is the source and guarantor of this covenant. And that's peace enough to carry on. This isn't Hallmark greeting card peace but real peace for the storm that's brewing. The covenant provides this.

A few years ago a Beijing police officer made the news while responding to a suicide attempt. A woman was preparing to jump from a building. After talking with the woman, and becoming convinced that she would jump, the officer did the unthinkable. He handcuffed himself to her and threw the key off the building. They were tied together for better or worse.[3] A covenant works like that. It's more than a Bible, theology, or church word. It's a real, essential, and practical promise that gives us everything we need. It's God's promise and actions that keep us forever. It gives stability, faithfulness, and peace.

In fact, as good as David and Jonathan's covenant was, and it was great, Jesus promises us a better one. That woman on the edge of the building saw the officer's love and backed down. But Jesus doesn't just handcuff himself to you on the ledge, he does so as you're free falling out of a plane, and he saves you by taking the fall for you and giving you life. This is the covenant. No matter what is going on in your life, the cuffs never come off. Jesus has you. You are secure.

Pause for a Moment

Reflect: Where, if anywhere, have you seen the idea of covenant played out in your life?

Request: Ask Jesus to give you increased faithfulness to others because of the ways in which his faithfulness has blessed and kept you.

Respond: Keep your vows today. Honor your vows to God, your spouse, your children, your parents, and those you serve.

And David rose and fled that day from Saul and went to Achish the king of Gath. And the servants of Achish said to him, "Is not this David the king of the land? Did they not sing to one another of him in dances, 'Saul has struck down his thousands, and David his ten thousands'?" And David took these words to heart and was much afraid of Achish the king of Gath. So he changed his behavior before them and pretended to be insane in their hands and made marks on the doors of the gate and let his spittle run down his beard. Then Achish said to his servants, "Behold, you see the man is mad. Why then have you brought him to me. . . Shall this fellow come into my house?" David departed from there and escaped to the cave of Adullam. And when his brothers and all his father's house heard it, they went down there to him. And everyone who was in distress, and everyone who was in debt, and everyone who was bitter in soul, gathered to him. And he became commander over them. And there were with him about four hundred men. And David went from there to Mizpeh of Moab. And he said to the king of Moab, "Please let my father and my mother stay with you, till I know what God will do for me." And he left them with the king of Moab, and they stayed with him all the time that David was in the stronghold. Then the prophet Gad said to David, "Do not remain in the stronghold; depart, and go into the land of Judah." So David departed and went into the forest of Hereth.

(1 Samuel 21:10–22:5)

6

THE STRUGGLE

(1 Samuel 21:10–22:5)

Growing up, my dad corrected my school papers and forced me to look up misspelled words in the dictionary. Not with spell check, not with dictionary.com, but with a massive and dusty hardbound dictionary. I spent hours flipping angrily through that book. Why did he make me suffer in such a cruel and archaic way? Did I become a better speller? To some extent. But more importantly, I learned how to patiently slow down and fix a problem without giving up. While it's one thing to learn life lessons from a dictionary it's quite another to learn them through real suffering. When the terminal disease doesn't go into remission, when the drought doesn't end, when the relationship heals at a snail's pace, when you stay frustrated with God, what can really be gained?

At this point in his young life, David could write a best-seller about the struggles he's overcome in trying to escape from King Saul. He probably felt like he'd suffered more than his fair share. But Scripture reminds us that God uses all things for the good and growth of his people.[1] In the moments of continued struggle this statement remains true even when we can't see what God is up to. So how can we expect to grow in the wilderness of struggle?

Growing in Praise

It had become increasingly clear that David wasn't safe in Israel and of all places he flees to the Philistine town of Gath. Unfortunately, the moment David arrives he's recognized and the people begin singing that old country song about David killing his ten thousands. Of course, the dead in this song are the dead friends and family of the Philistines (including Goliath who was from Gath!) and so the Philistines are naturally unhappy. David realizes his mistake and, in desperation, acts like a mad-man hoping to prove that he's not really the giant-killer. By God's grace, it works.

Looking back, David realizes what a foolish and desperate situation he had put himself in. He responds by writing Psalms 34 and 56 where he's honest about his desperation, "my enemies trample on me all day long" and his hope, "The LORD is near the brokenhearted." David even ends with praise "I will bless the LORD at all times... Blessed is the man who takes refuge in him." In the struggle, David realized that God is the only one worthy of trust and praise. What if we too realized that our struggles didn't disqualify us from praising God or sharing his praise with others? What if the honest yet hopeful pain of Christians was a far better testimony to the world then stories about how our life is perfect?

Growing in Trust

Living in the struggle can also help us learn to trust God's plan. David gets a glimpse of this as we learn that God was working to meet David's needs 100 years prior to the events of this passage. As 1 Samuel 22 begins, David escapes from the Philistines and makes his way to a wilderness cave. His family, who were also in danger, arrive at the cave but there's a problem. His parents were too old for the outlaw lifestyle. David decides to take them to the King of Moab. As he does this, two interesting things happen: *"(David) said to the king of Moab, "Please let my father and my mother stay with you, till I know what God will do for me. And he left them with the king of Moab"* (22:3-4). First, David confesses that he doesn't know the future but that he knows God will provide. Second, this foreign king agrees to help David. Why? It's likely he was honoring a family connection. David is part Moabite by birth. His great grandmother was Ruth, a full-blooded Moabite whose life was dominated by suffering and God's redemption.[2] By saving Ruth years ago, God was saving the future king of Israel in more ways than one. In the obvious and the unseen, God's good plan was at work, even when David couldn't see it.

Growing In The Word

But what if you are in the midst of the struggle and praise and trust are hard to come by? David is given encouragement that every person reading this page can share in: *"Then the prophet Gad said to David, 'Do not remain in the stronghold; depart, and go into the land of Judah'"* (22:5). Out of nowhere, a little-known prophet finds David and speaks God's words to him, telling him what to do. It's just one verse in our story but the implications are huge. For one, David has God's guidance and his enemy Saul does not. For another, David can trust in God's direction. In the darkest struggle, the Lord is not silent.

That's swell for David you might think. How convenient to get a clear word from a prophet. Lucky David. But we forgot, David had far less of God's Word than we do. We have the whole story, in our hands, accurately translated in our language, with complete access anytime we pick up our Bible or smartphone. We all wish we heard God audibly on a regular basis, but we forget that what we have is actually better. The Apostle Peter reminds us of this when he says, "we have the prophetic word more fully confirmed, to which you will do well to pay attention as to a lamp shining in a dark place."[3] We might argue that our situation isn't changing, and that God seems silent and absent. But he's not. In the wilderness of struggle God is wooing us, whispering to us, and even shouting to us with his Word. Take it and read. And as you read this particular story, we are given even more hope.

Indeed, as David suffered, something amazing happened for other struggling people. *"And everyone who was in distress, and everyone who was in debt, and everyone who was bitter in soul gathered to [David]"* (22:2). God provided for David in his struggle so that he could care for other strugglers. Our Greater David came to do the same. You don't have to get your act together, achieve the perfect life, or even understand your suffering to rest in Jesus. In fact, the opposite is true. All you need is enough struggle, dissatisfaction, and desperation to come and rest at the feet of Him who has suffered so that he can gather a people to himself.

Pause for a Moment

Reflect: Is it natural for you to think about suffering as a tool that God uses for our good? Why or why not?

Request: If you are not deeply struggling today thank God for his provision and ask him to make you ready for whatever lies ahead. If you are, ask God to help your praise become battle-tested, your trust in his unseen hand more sure, and your reliance upon the Word more desperate.

Respond: Throughout the day, look for people who are desperate, bitter, or suffering. Remember that Jesus is gathering such a people as this to himself and find a practical way to encourage, get to know, or simply make contact with them.

Then Saul took three thousand chosen men. . . and went to seek David. . . And he came to the sheepfolds by the way, where there was a cave, and Saul went in to relieve himself. Now David and his men were sitting in the innermost parts of the cave. And the men of David said to him, "Here is the day of which the LORD said to you, 'Behold, I will give your enemy into your hand, and you shall do to him as it shall seem good to you.' " Then David arose and stealthily cut off a corner of Saul's robe. And afterward David's heart struck him. . . He said to his men, "The LORD forbid that I should do this thing to my lord, the LORD's anointed. . ." Afterward. . . [he] called after Saul. . . And. . .bowed. . . "Why do you listen to the words of men who say, 'Behold, David seeks your harm'? Behold, this day your eyes have seen how the LORD gave you today into my hand. . . And some told me to kill you, but I spared you. . . For by the fact that I cut off the corner of your robe and did not kill you, you may know and see that there is no wrong or treason in my hands. I have not sinned against you, though you hunt my life to take it. May the LORD judge between me and you, may the LORD avenge me against you, but my hand shall not be against you. . ." And Saul. . . said to David, "You are more righteous than I, for you have repaid me good, whereas I have repaid you evil. . . So may the LORD reward you with good for what you have done to me this day. And now, behold, I know that you shall surely be king, and that the kingdom of Israel shall be established in your hand. . ."

(1 Samuel 24: 2–20)

7

SHORTCUT

(1 Samuel 24)

Let me share with you some humbling realities about the American Church. The Apostle Paul commands God's people to be generous with their money yet only 10% tithe according to Scriptural guidelines.[1] In the Psalms, King David tells us that we need God's Word for daily living yet only 20% of Christians read the Bible daily.[2] Jesus tells us that we must share the gospel with others yet only 40% of Christians have shared anything about their faith with an unbeliever in the past six months.[3] Of course, we've got our excuses. We don't give because the budget is tight, we don't read because we're busy, and we don't share our faith because it's awkward. We think we know best. We trust our wisdom over the Word of God. We'd never say it like this, but our actions speak louder than our words. The truth is, as the Church, we're a broken group of people who still wrestle with trusting ourselves more than God.

This is why we need 1 Samuel 24. We need to remember the importance of trusting God's way. King David's son Solomon stated this truth well when he said, "Trust in the LORD with all your heart and do not lean on your own understanding."[4] This cry is repeated throughout Scripture. But it's easier said than done. As David continues his time in the wilderness he's going to be given a tantalizing opportunity to do things his way and make his life easier once and for all. Let's find out how David's temptation can help us learn to trust God.

Is God's Way Always Right?

Sometimes temptation hits us when we're least expecting it. Here's the situation: King Saul is on a hunting expedition for David and decides to take a bathroom break. As he's taking care of his business in a cave we learn that David and a few of his men are hiding right behind him. David's men instantly see this as a wonderful opportunity from God to kill Saul: *"And the men... Said to him, "Here is the day of which the LORD said to you, "Behold, I will give your enemy into your hand, and you shall do to him as it shall seem good to you"* (24:4). David's men were partially right: God had led Saul to this compromising position and he had promised to make David King.[5] But the men were also wrong: God hadn't given David permission to do whatever he wanted, and he hadn't promised David anything specific about Saul's demise. The men were tempting David with an enticing half-truth. I can imagine them saying, "Look David, we're no prophets, but you're good, Saul's evil, and look, here he is, just one little stab and all your problems will be gone, what a nice gift from God!" The best temptations are always based on half-truths as Adam and Eve discovered in Eden. Complete lies are often far too easy to spot and far too hard to justify.

David wavers and settles for cutting off part of Saul's robe as proof of this opportunity and as a symbol of his power over

Saul. Instantly, David feels regret. Why? *"[David] said to his men, "The LORD forbid that I should do this thing to my lord, the LORD's anointed. . ."*(24:6) Though God had declared that Saul had lost his blessing, God had not yet removed him from his position. Saul was still set apart by God for the special role of King. To curse or attack Saul was to do the same to God. David refuses the shortcut and will wait for God. As Christians today, we are offered millions of shortcuts in every area of life. Can we recognize them, especially when they are *almost* right and *almost* what God wants?

Does God's Way Always Bring Us Peace?

The anticipated peace of a Saul-free world must have weighed heavily upon David. However, as he obeyed, David found satisfaction in knowing that he had not sinned in his relationship with Saul. After Saul finishes his business, David calls out to him from a distance and, through the strength that God alone supplies, demonstrates respect and honor to the man who was seeking to kill him.

This doesn't mean that everything is right between David and Saul or that it's now safe for David to come home. It's not. But it does mean that David can have peace knowing that he's right with Saul on his end of the relationship: *"there is no wrong or treason on my hands. I have not sinned against you"* (24:11). More importantly, David is able to share with Saul the peace that obedience to God brings: *"May the LORD therefore be judge and give sentence between me and you, and see to it and plead my cause and deliver me from your hand"* (24:15). David has no control over Saul's response but he can rest in the confidence of knowing that he is right with the One who really matters.

Is God's Way Really Fair?

We serve a God who is fully just. And surely the death of a wicked king seemed fair to David. Was sparing Saul really a way to achieve justice? Yes. David knew it just wouldn't be on his schedule: *"May the LORD judge between me and you, may the LORD avenge me against you, but my hand shall not be against you"* (20:12). Paul puts it this way in the New Testament: "Beloved, never avenge yourselves, but leave it to the wrath of God, for it is written, 'Vengeance is mine, I will repay, says the LORD'."[6] David can let God take care of justice just as Paul calls believers to do the same today.

David's peaceful response shocks King Saul. He can no longer deny that God must be at work in David: *"And now, behold, I know that you shall surely be king, and that the kingdom of Israel shall be established in your hand"* (24:20). This is a foretaste of eternity when all God's enemies will admit that God's hero is King. And this is good news for us. Like David, we don't have to do things our way. We can trust that the greater King David, who sits at the right hand of the Father with sword in hand, is ready to defend us from every temptation and adversary.[7] He will get the last word. He did when he stood toe to toe with the snake of hell and dealt the decisive blow on the cross. His way is right, it brings peace, and it brings justice. Trust in him.

Pause for a Moment

Reflect: In what area of your life are you most tempted to take shortcuts?

Request: Ask God to fight for you the next time you feel tempted. Trust that Jesus' work on the cross proves his power *and* love for you.

Respond: After God reveals your preferred shortcuts, do the hard work of doing the right thing and waiting for the only peace that lasts. Jesus promises you enough grace to do so.

*The man was very rich. . . the name of the man was Nabal, and
the name of his wife Abigail. The woman was discerning and
beautiful, but the man was harsh and badly behaved. . . David
heard. . . that Nabal was shearing his sheep. So David sent ten
young men. And. . . said. . . "Thus you shall greet him: 'Peace be
to you. . . your shepherds have been with us, and we did them
no harm. . .we come on a feast day. Please give whatever you
have at hand to your servants and to your son David'". . . And
Nabal answered. . . "Who is David? . . . There are many
servants these days who are breaking away from their
masters. Shall I take my bread. . . and give it to men who come
from I do not know where?". . . And David said to his men,
"Every man strap on his sword!". . . Then Abigail made haste. . .
When Abigail saw David. . . She fell at his feet and said, ". . . Let
not my lord regard this worthless fellow, Nabal. . . Now. . .
because the LORD has restrained you. . . let your enemies and
those who seek to do evil to my lord be as Nabal. . .For the
LORD will certainly make my lord a sure house. . . " And David
said . . . "Blessed be the LORD, the God of Israel, who sent you
this day to meet me! Blessed be your discretion, and blessed be
you, who have kept me this day from bloodguilt and from
working salvation with my own hand!". . . And Abigail came to
Nabal, and behold, he was holding a feast in his house. . . In the
morning, when the wine had gone out of Nabal, his wife told
him these things, and his heart died within him, and he
became as a stone. And about ten days later the LORD struck
Nabal, and he died. . . Then David sent and spoke to Abigail, to
take her as his wife.*
(1 Samuel 25:2–39)

IDENTITY CRISIS

(1 Samuel 25)

Growing up in Kansas City, I was automatically a Royals fan. However, this baseball loyalty was fiercely tested when I moved to St. Louis for seminary. At this point in time I'd never seen the Royals play winning baseball and the St. Louis baseball experience, with their beautiful downtown stadium, their winning teams and traditions, and a city full of die-hard fans, was hard not to like. I was truly tested when the Royals came to town. Would I wear Royal blue or Cardinal red? Was I willing to stand out as a faithful outsider or was I willing to fit in as a traitor? Which team would I identify with?

It can be pretty tempting to forget our identity. We've all had moments where we didn't want to be associated with a particular friend, our line of work, our hometown, or even our last name. But let's cut to the chase and ask the harder question: have you ever wanted to hide that fact that you're a Christian? I have. Be real, haven't you? Has it happened in specific moments or has it been a gradual distancing from Christ? A lot of situations can push us in this direction: a new set of friends or coworkers, the start of college, or a major family tragedy. The temptation to forget our identity is real.

David grappled with this very issue as his time in the wilderness staggered on. Thankfully, words of truth and grace were spoken to him at just the right time. He was reminded that he was a child of God. We too must remember this. But how?

Spiritual Orphans

Over the last several months, David and his band of outcasts had provided free protection for the cattlemen whose herds grazed in the wilderness. David learned that one of these cattlemen, Nabal, was throwing a feast and David asked the man for some leftovers. The request was important not only because David had been serving this man for free, but also because hospitality was seen as the ultimate expression of love in the ancient Near East. Hospitality revealed a person's character and Nabal's response was shocking. He not only said no, but he also insulted the work and person of David.

We should have expected this. Nabal's name means "foolish", and this man's wife, servants, King David, and the writer of 1 Samuel all label him as such in this chapter. Nabel found his identity in his possessions and the greed he used to clutch them tightly. Nabal was a spiritual orphan. He rejected his heavenly Father and lived as if the world was created simply for his own selfish desires. Nabal was his own god.

Nabal's venom not only offended David, it also began to poison him. David displayed a very human knee-jerk reaction. *"David said. . . 'Every man strap on his sword. . . God do so to the enemies of David and more also, if by morning I leave so much as one male of all who belong to him'"* (25:13 & 22). Like Nabal, David found himself swept into the position of God. He forgot who he was and Whose he was. And all this happens to David as a child of God. The same happens to us. We hear the poisonous lies of spiritual orphan-hood and function as if we are without a heavenly Father. Fortunately, our enemy can't actually make us orphans. Unfortunately, he can encourage us to live like ones. That's what's happening to David.

Children of God

So how does David remember who he is? Someone else speaks truth to him. David meets Abigail, a consummate child of God. The situation unfolds as Abigail hears about her husband's selfish and foolish decision to insult David. She quickly packs provisions and sends them ahead to David. When she arrives, she apologizes and encourages David to disregard Nabal.

Most importantly, Abigail calls David to remember his identity as a child of God: *"The LORD will certainly make my lord a sure house. . . and evil shall not be found in you as long as you live. If men rise up to pursue you and to seek your life, the life of my lord shall be bound in the bundle of the living in the care of the LORD your God. And the lives of your enemies he shall sling out as from the hollow of a sling"* (25:28–29). Abigail risks her life encouraging David to remember who he is in God. David is not God. David is also not the bloodthirsty murderer of foolish old men. He is a child of God, a child dependent on the God who saved him from the giant (notice the reference to the sling) and who has promised him a sure future.

Abigail's loving risk reaps an unimaginable reward. By the grace of God, Abigail sets the future king and forefather of Jesus back on track, and David knows it. He praises God's work through her. David won't have to kill Nabal. He doesn't have to get even. He's a child of God and God, not sin, will give David what he needs. Like David, we have to replace the lies of spiritual orphan-hood with the truths of God. We are not alone. We are children of the living God. His care is enough.

I ended up going to that Cardinals game with another life-long Royals fan. We took off our jackets as we found our seats. I proudly displayed my Royal blue. Shockingly, my friend revealed a red shirt. He'd hidden his identity! Sadly, I heckled him for his faithlessness for the rest of the night, deeply hurting his feelings and wounding our friendship. That night I'd remembered my identity as a Royals fan but forgotten my identity as a child of God. I was no hero.

Today, David was no hero either. In his pride, David forgot who he was and found himself sucked into the lies of orphan-hood. Despite this, God sent a brave woman to speak truth to him and pull him back from the edge. The story ends with Nabal dying of a stroke when he learns how much his wife gave David and how close David came to killing him. Abigail ends up marrying David.[1] Despite David's failure, God's plan works out, justice is served, and David and Abigail are blessed. We don't need to be more like David, we're already too much like him in our sin. We need a leader who can deal with the jeers of a thousand Nabals and stay the course. We need a leader who not only can make us into children of God but who can also help us remember it every day. We need Jesus.

Pause for a Moment

Reflect: What lies of spiritual orphan-hood do you hear the most?

Request: Ask God to provide Abigails in your life to remind you that you are a child of God.

Respond: Find a brother or sister in Christ today and remind them of who they are in Christ specifically in a way that will encourage them in whatever struggles or challenges they are facing.

Then David said in his heart, "Now I shall perish one day by the hand of Saul. There is nothing better for me than that I should escape to the land of the Philistines..." So David arose and went over, he and the six hundred men who were with him, to Achish... King of Gath... And when it was told Saul that David had fled to Gath, he no longer sought him. Then David said to Achish, "If I have found favor in your eyes, let a place be given me in one of the country towns, that I may dwell there..." So that day Achish gave him Ziklag... Now David and his men went up and made raids against the Geshurites, the Girzites, and the Amalekites, for these were the inhabitants of the land from of old... And David would strike the land and would leave neither man nor woman alive, but would take away the sheep, the oxen, the donkeys, the camels, and the garments, and come back to Achish. When Achish asked, "Where have you made a raid today?" David would say, "Against the Negeb of Judah"... And David would leave neither man nor woman alive to bring news to Gath, thinking, "lest they should tell about us and say, 'So David has done.'" Such was his custom all the while he lived in the country of the Philistines. And Achish trusted David, thinking, "He has made himself an utter stench to his people Israel; therefore he shall always be my servant"... the Philistines gathered their forces for war, to fight against Israel. And Achish said to David, "Understand that you and your men are to go out with me in the army." David said to Achish, "Very well, you shall know what your servant can do."

(1 Samuel 27:1–28:2)

9

THE MUCK AND THE MIRE

(1 Samuel 27–28:2)

In what types of situations can we expect to hear from God? Here's how Sarah's morning went last Monday: The sun was rising beautifully as Sarah awoke. She lit a candle. There was no rush. A peaceful breeze blew in from her kitchen window as she turned on quiet Christian music. Her children were still asleep. The house was spotless, the bills paid, and everyone was healthy. She smiled and opened her Bible to read God's Word. Now here's how Sarah's morning went *this* Monday: The sun burst into Sarah's eyes as her alarm clock exploded with a shrill cry. She could smell dirty diapers wafting across the room. Soon, the sound of children fighting and orange juice spilling on the floor moved her into action. She had 50 things to get done. She had a cold. She had argued with her husband the night before about finances, and now she was late getting the kids to school.

In which situation could Sarah most expect to experience God? Why do we answer this question so quickly? Let's slow ourselves down for a moment and reflect. Don't we struggle to believe that God works in the messiness of life? Do you think differently? Do we really believe that God is present in the rush, stress, anxiety, and dysfunction of everyday life? Doesn't He expect something different from us? Can we expect to find Him in messes that we've created? Can we expect His presence when we've forgotten about him or haven't been a model believer? After another close brush with King Saul, David finds his life in such a messy blur that God isn't even mentioned in 1 Samuel 27. And yet, God is at work because he, not David, is the hero. As David sings in Psalm 68: "Our God is a God who saves." And for God to save, we would have to need saving. And we do. So how does God meet us in the messiness of life?

The Messiness of Fear

One of things that makes our lives messy is fear. A quick recap of David's life reminds us that he's lost his hard-earned position and reputation in Israel, he's lost his first wife, he's been betrayed, lied to, and hunted like an animal, all while living in the wilderness. The exhaustion of it all certainly took a huge toll on David, and he began to listen to the lies of fear. *"Then David said in his heart, 'Now I shall perish one day by the hand of Saul. There is nothing better for me than that I should escape to the land of the Philistines' "* (27:1). The word *perish* refers to being swept away or doomed. The glass is certainly empty in David's mind.

Listening to fear, David turns to a man-made solution, and a poor one at that. Because it worked so well the first time (it didn't), David decides to once again run away to the nation of his enemies, Philistia. Instead of waiting with patience and trust, fear can quickly push us down a messy path of rushed decisions and self-reliance.

The Messiness of Pride

If fear tells us that we're doomed, then pride tells us that we can (or should try to) fix our problems. As contradictory as these two thoughts sound, they surprisingly go hand in hand when life gets messy. After letting fear rush him to Philistia, David begins to think that he's got a handle on his new living situation.

The Philistines surprisingly accept David this time around, and Saul gives up the hunt. David asks for and receives a small town for his men to live in. He begins raiding Israel's enemies to make ends meet but lies to King Achish about it by telling him that the spoils are coming from Israel. David thinks that he can trust his enemies enough to live with them while using lies and violence to pretend that he's betraying his own people. As Proverbs puts it, "There is a way that seems right to a man, but its end is the way to death."[1] David is treading on dangerous ground.

A Messy Mess

David's plan works too well. The Philistine warlords decide to renew a massive military campaign against Israel and, because of his fear and pride-inspired lies, David is asked to join his enemies in killing his own countrymen. *"And Achish said to David, 'Understand that you and your men are to go out with me in the army. David said to Achish, 'Very well, you shall know what your servant can do.' "* (28:1–2) David had found himself in a fine mess. He was being called to fight Israel, and there could be no faking it this time. If he fought Israel he'd be breaking his covenant as the future king of Israel, and he would become a true traitor against God and his people. If he refused, he'd likely face death from the Philistines for deserting and tricking their king. His kingship, and the hope and safety of Israel, not to mention the bloodline of the future Messiah, all rested on David's answer. His mess had finally caught up with him. All David can do is give a vague answer while scrambling to fix this self-inflicted disaster.

Has David disappointed you today? After inspiring you with courage, humility, and faith are you surprised by his sin? Are you more upset that Scripture shares this story or that God chose a man to be his king who was this calculating, dishonest, and ruthless? If you feel any of that, realize that it's coming from the same part of you that struggles to believe that God is present in the messiness of life.

In part, God gave us this story to correct our tendency to worship Bible heroes.[2] We picture them as perfect, attractive, and sanitized, but they are often broken, dishonest, rough, repentance-needing sinners. What we must realize is that there is no other type of person. God works in messiness because this life is a mess. God will overcome David's fear, pride, and the resulting mess because that's what God does in the lives of all his children. After all, there's only one hero worthy of our worship, one hero who won't let us down, and one hero who won't leave us in our mess without hope. That hero is Jesus, and his gospel teaches us that even in our mess, he has loved us, saved us, and promised to never leave us. There's hope for the mess.

Pause for a Moment

Reflect: In what situations do you find yourself assuming that God isn't present?

Request: Ask God to show you which people in your life, history, or Scripture that you've elevated into super-human status. Ask him to remind you that there are only grace-needing people because there's only one hero, Jesus.

Respond: Share a current struggle in your life with another person who respects you as a way to humble yourself and encourage them to see you as fully human.

Now the Philistines had gathered all their forces at Aphek. And the Israelites were encamped by the spring that is in Jezreel... the commanders of the Philistines said, "What are these Hebrews doing here?" And Achish said... "Is this not David... Who has been with me now for days and years, and since he deserted to me I have found no fault in him to this day." But the commanders of the Philistines were angry with him. And... said to him, "Send the man back, that he may return to the place to which you have assigned him. He shall not go down with us to battle, lest in the battle he become an adversary to us... Is not this David, of whom they sing to one another in dances, 'Saul has struck down his thousands, and David his ten thousands'?" Then Achish called David and said to him, "As the LORD lives, you have been honest, and to me it seems right that you should march out and in with me in the campaign. For I have found nothing wrong in you... Nevertheless, the lords do not approve of you. So go back now...." And David said to Achish, "But what have I done?... " And Achish answered David and said, "I know that you are as blameless in my sight as an angel of God. Nevertheless, the commanders of the Philistines have said, 'He shall not go up with us to the battle.' Now then rise early in the morning with the servants of your lord who came with you... and depart as soon as you have light." So David set out with his men early in the morning to return to the land of the Philistines...

(1 Samuel 29)

10

DELIVERED

(1 Samuel 29)

Spring was beginning, and it was time to give some much-needed attention to my lawn. One particular goal was reseeding a bare patch in front of the house. I roughed up the soil, laid down the seed with a new soil mixture that was supposed to protect it, and watered it twice daily. Then I waited. Nothing happened. I began to worry when I saw birds picking at the new soil. Then the wind blew some of it away. It rained. Then it got dry. Was it ruined? I waited and waited. No evidence of growth. Had I been ripped off? Had I done something wrong? How could I know?

How do we know if God is working in our lives? We can't see him, most of us haven't heard him audibly, and most of us haven't seen a dramatic miracle such as the blind seeing or the deaf hearing. So how do we know? David himself was probably asking this question. In the last chapter we discussed the mess he had made in his life through his fear and pride-influenced decisions. Even so, we stated that God surely is at work in the lives of messy and broken people. In the New Testament, Jesus criticized his opponents for ever thinking that there was a time when God was not at work.[1] Once God makes a person his child, the Apostle Paul tells us, he never stops working in their lives.[2] We know that all of this true. But in the midst of it all, what can we be looking for? Some grand sign? A gentle whisper of hope?

A Subtle God

A quick recap from the previous chapter: David, filled with fear, has fled from King Saul back into the land of the Philistines. This time around they accepted him, gave him and his men a small town to live in, and are under the (false) impression that David was spending his time making raids against his own people Israel. Worse yet, the Philistines are preparing for a major campaign against Israel, and they want David to fight for them. To do so would be treason against his people and God. To refuse would mean death from the Philistines. David is in a jam.

Nevertheless, God is at work in the background. His name is not mentioned in this chapter (again!) except once from the lips of the Philistine king. There is no major miracle, God does not speak audibly, and yet David is rescued. He will not have to fight Israel, he is not discovered as a double agent, he's let off the hook, and it's all because the Philistine kings have a disagreement. This is not luck. Though it is not spelled out, this is divine deliverance. God has never left David in the past, and he has not left him now: God is at work even in the background.

We see this throughout the Bible as God speaks to the prophet Elijah not in the wind, an earthquake, or blazing fire, but in the stillness.[3] The people of Judah will later return from exile not because of a great military victory but because of a pagan king's edict.[4] Jesus himself says that his kingdom is like a small seed that grows into a large tree, like a little yeast that leavens an entire loaf.[5] God's work is often subtle, but it's always good. Are you missing God's work in your life because you're looking for something extravagant or Hollywood-esqe? Maybe it's time to look at the little things.

A Surprising God

Think about how God saved David. Help doesn't come from within David as if he could fight his way to safety and it doesn't come from a trusted source like his friend Jonathan. No, David is saved out of his own mess by enemy warlords.

Here's the scene. The five Philistine kings are meeting up to unite forces to attack Israel and the other four lords spot David with King Achish and throw a fit. *"The commanders of the Philistines were angry with [Achish]. And [they] said to him, 'Send the man back... He shall not go down with us to battle, lest in the battle he become an adversary to us... Is not this David of whom they sing to one another in dances, 'Saul has struck down his thousands, and David his ten thousands?'"* (29:4–5). It's that old country song again. But this time, David is saved at the mention of it. The Philistine kings wisely want nothing to do with David and send him packing.

Again, this shouldn't shock us. God surprisingly saved David earlier in life from Saul's attacks by letting the Philistines invade.[6] In the New Testament, God uses the great evil and betrayal of the disciple Judas and the resulting death of Jesus on a cross to save his people.[7] God's work is often surprising, and it's always good. Are you prepared to see God at work in the surprising or even the painful?

A Gracious God

Did David deserve anything that God provided him in this passage? No. He was in this mess because of his own fear, pride, and lies. He was saved by God's grace from fighting his countrymen, breaking his covenant with the Lord, and being discovered as a double agent.

Sadly, King Achish was so duped by David's lies that he refers to David as a *"blameless... angel of God."*(29:9) We know that's not the case. Worse yet, David almost digs himself another hole by protesting his dismissal. While this was possibly one final calculated acting job, it was far too risky and David was fortunate the Philistine Kings didn't change their mind. God saves him from all these things purely out of grace. And this is how God always works. The Apostle Paul reminds us that "it depends not on human will or exertion, but on God, who has mercy"[8] and "for by grace you have been saved through faith. And this is not your own doing, it is the gift of God."[9] God is often subtle, often surprising, but always gracious.

After days of anxious waiting and doubting, I awoke one sunny morning and walked by that empty patch of grass. Hundreds of little, but good-looking shoots were filling the patch even though it had been empty the night before. The seeds had been growing and working the whole time and finally had exploded out of the protective soil. I should have known that grass always works like that. The same is true of God. As demonstrated most wonderfully in the Second David's death on the cross, God's work is not prone to grace, it is gracious. We should expect the subtle and surprising. But we can count on grace every time we think about our Savior's work in our lives.

Pause for a Moment

Reflect: When has God worked in your life in surprising and subtle ways?

Request: Confess your tendency to think that God owes you answered prayers and help. Rest in the fact that Jesus' death has purchased God's grace for you.

Respond: Believe that God is at work in your life today, especially when you can't see it.

Now when David and his men came to Ziklag... the Amalekites had made a raid... They had... burned it with fire and taken captive the women and all who were in it... Then David and the people who were with him raised their voices and wept until they had no more strength to weep... And David was greatly distressed, for the people spoke of stoning him, because all the people were bitter in soul, each for his sons and daughters. But David strengthened himself in the LORD his God. And David said to Abiathar the priest... "Bring me the ephod"... And David inquired of the LORD, "Shall I pursue after this band?"... He answered him, "Pursue, for you shall surely overtake and shall surely rescue." So, David set out... and they came to the brook Besor... Two hundred stayed behind, who were too exhausted to cross the brook Besor. They found an Egyptian in the open country and brought him to David... And David said to him, "Will you take me down to this band?"... And when he had taken him down, behold, they were spread abroad... eating and drinking and dancing... And David struck them down from twilight until the evening of the next day... David recovered all that the Amalekites had taken, and David rescued his two wives...

David brought back all... Then David came to the two hundred men who had been too exhausted to follow... who had been left at the brook Besor... Then all the wicked and worthless fellows among the men who had gone with David said, "Because they did not go with us, we will not give them any of the spoil..."But David said, "You shall not do so, my brothers, with what the LORD has given us. He has preserved us and given into our hand the band that came against us..."

(1 Samuel 30:1–23)

11

SEARCH AND RESCUE

(1 Samuel 30)

Frequently we find ourselves in need of strength to carry on. Who hasn't found themselves running on fumes, burnt-out, empty, and desperate for some strength? In 1 Samuel 30, David desperately needed help and so do we, perhaps far more than we know. So what are we to do? There's only one viable answer. We must seek God's strength. In Psalm 63 David puts it this way, "Earnestly I seek you, my soul thirsts for you, my flesh faints for you." We must be desperate for God and the Apostle Paul reminds us why, "Not that we are sufficient in ourselves... But our sufficiency is from God."[1] How does this make a practical difference in our lives?

Strength in the Day of Disaster

David and his men had taken a long three-day journey back from the Philistine war camp to their Philistine home in Ziklag. Covering roughly twenty-five miles a day in a harsh environment, the men were surely tired and longing for a home-cooked meal. But it was not to be. Ziklag was burned. Raiders had attacked the unguarded city and taken the men's families, likely as slaves for work and pleasure. The men were gutted. *"[They] raised their voices and wept until they had no more strength to weep"* (30:4). After the initial shock wore off, the men turned their frustration towards David. *"the people spoke of stoning [David], because all the people were bitter in soul, each for his sons and daughters"* (30:6). David was in a tough spot. What could he do? Could he save the day?

The movie *Taken* tells the story of a retired CIA agent who is forced to rescue his kidnapped daughter. There's an especially dramatic scene when the father gets his daughter's kidnapper on the phone. The conversation goes like this: "I don't know who you are. I don't know what you want. If you're looking for ransom I can tell you I don't have money. But what I do have are a very particular set of skills. Skills I have acquired over a very long career (in the CIA). Skills that make me a nightmare for people like you. If you let my daughter go now, that'll be the end of it. . . but if you don't I will look for you. I will find you. And I will kill you." The rest of the movie is about the father doing this very thing: rescuing his daughter and killing her captors.[2]

Isn't this what we want David to do? But this isn't a movie. David *can't* save the day. Instead, he does the one thing he can do. *"But David strengthened himself in the LORD his God"* (30:6). The day of disaster had struck and all David could do was turn to his God. Yet this was everything. David *was* strengthened. And it was only possible because he personally knew the Lord. Do you?

Strength in the Difficulty of Decisions

David is encouraged but can he find and recover the captives? Thankfully, David remembers that God has provided him with a priest.[3] *"And David said to Abiathar the priest. . . 'Bring me the ephod'[4]. . . And David inquired of the LORD, 'Shall I pursue after this band?'. . . He answered him, 'Pursue, for you shall surely overtake and shall surely rescue'"* (30:7–8). David secures God's guidance through God's gracious provision.

Next, when David heads in the general direction of the raiders, he leaves those who are too tired behind at the brook of Besor (this will be important later). As David continues the rescue mission God provides him with even more guidance. David and his men discover an Egyptian slave who has been left behind by the raiders. David persuades the slave to guide him to the enemies. Again, God provides what is needed. Are you wrestling with difficult decisions? Do you wish you had access to a priest like David? Remember, as a child of God, you have access to a priest far better than Abiathar in Jesus Christ who sits at the right hand of God and guarantees you access to God's strength and direction.

Strength for Every Act of Obedience

David and his men discovered the raiders basking in the spoils of their plundering. Now it was time for David to obey God by freeing the captives and destroying the kidnappers. Despite being exhausted and outnumbered, God provides a complete and resounding victory: *"Nothing was missing, whether small or great, sons or daughters, spoil or anything that had been taken. David brought back all"* (30:18–19). But God's not done. After the "big" battle, a "small" battle arises that requires David's continued obedience. Some wicked men among David's troops made a selfish request. They wanted to withhold the recovered possessions from the men who had been left behind at the Brook Besor. This was to be a punishment for their inability to fight. It seemed small, but much was at stake: *"You shall not do so, my brothers, with what the LORD has given us. He has preserved us. . . For as his share is who goes down into the battle, so shall his share be who stays by the baggage. They shall share alike"* (30:23–24). David knew that God had provided the victory. How could anyone selfishly claim for himself what God had given in grace? Their identity was in God, not personal performance.

So what about you? Are you stuck in a day of disaster? Are you worn down and weary? Do you feel too tired to press on even though you've prayed, read your Bible, and tried to trust God?

Remember what King David does for the weary men who were left behind at the brook. Instead of shaming them, he greeted them in peace. This reminds us of another David who said, "Come to me, all who labor and are heavy laden, and I will give you rest."[5] After greeting the tired men, David divides the spoils evenly. This too reminds us of the greater David who spoke of a master who hired men to work at different times throughout the day and yet paid them all evenly saying, "Am I not allowed to do what I choose with what belongs to me."[6] King David's victory was complete and decisive. The Greater King's victory is sure and we who wait beside that brook, the worn out and weary, will get to share in that victory even though He did all the fighting. No matter how tired you are there is a brook where you can rest and receive strength and blessing undeserved. That brook is Christ.

Pause for a Moment

Reflect: What situation is currently wearing you down the most?

Request: Ask Jesus to show you the goodness of acting when he calls you to act and resting when he calls you to rest.

Respond: Take a moment to celebrate. Eat your favorite food, drink your favorite drink, sing your favorite song, or take a moment to rest. Jesus has won the war. You might be in the middle of the day of disaster, but Jesus will bring you out. You can celebrate now.

Now the Philistines were fighting against Israel, and the men of Israel fled before the Philistines and fell slain on Mount Gilboa. And the Philistines overtook Saul and his sons, and. . . struck down Jonathan and Abinadab and Malchi-shua, the sons of Saul. The battle pressed hard against Saul, and the archers found him, and he was badly wounded. . . Then Saul said to his armor-bearer, "Draw your sword, and thrust me through with it, lest these uncircumcised come and thrust me through, and mistreat me." But his armor-bearer would not, for he feared greatly. Therefore Saul took his own sword and fell upon it. . . Thus Saul died, and his three sons, and his armor-bearer, and all his men, on the same day together. And when the men of Israel. . . saw that the men of Israel had fled and that Saul and his sons were dead, they abandoned their cities and fled. And the Philistines came and lived in them. The next day, when the Philistines came to strip the slain, they found Saul and his three sons fallen on Mount Gilboa. So they cut off his head and stripped off his armor and sent messengers throughout the land of the Philistines, to carry the good news to the house of their idols and to the people. They put his armor in the temple of Ashtaroth, and they fastened his body to the wall of Beth-shan. But when the inhabitants of Jabesh-gilead heard what the Philistines had done to Saul, all the valiant men arose and went all night and took the body of Saul and the bodies of his sons from the wall of Beth-shan, and they came to Jabesh and burned them there. And they took their bones and buried them under the tamarisk tree in Jabesh and fasted seven days.

(1 Samuel 31)

12

FAILURE

(1 Samuel 31)

My favorite day-to-day shoes are Sanuks. There's a lot to love about these semi-casual shoes with their wide cushy soles (I promise this isn't paid advertising). Anyway, I rarely took off my first pair. I wore them without socks, rain or shine, even while taking a canoe down a river. Sadly, everything I loved about the shoes began to disappear. I tore a hole in the side and they became too wide. They stopped looking or smelling casual. I wore through the sole and began to feel the pavement on my heel. What could be done? Like a good American consumer, I tossed them in the trash and ordered more.

It's one thing to ditch and replace a product that no longer works, but what happens when the people of God fail? Can we throw the Church out? What happens when leaders fail, the Church hurts your feelings, or closes its doors? It's natural to feel anger, apathy, or devastation. In 1 Samuel 31, the people of God utterly fail. Specifically, their leader, King Saul, fails morally and physically. What can Israel do? Psalm 62 tells them, "Trust in him at all times, O people. Pour out your heart before him. God is a refuge for us." Paul echoes this in Ephesians 5 when he reminds us that Christ died to save the Church, the people of God. The Lord has and always will continue to save his Church. Let's examine the situations that tempt us most to forget this:

When Leaders Fail

King Saul found himself in a desperate situation as the Philistines attacked: *"The battle pressed hard against Saul... and he was badly wounded by the archers... Therefore Saul took his own sword and fell upon it"* (31:3–4). How did Saul end up here? He'd made a habit of disobeying God and failing to repent. God warned that judgment was coming. Now, tragically, Saul fulfills this by killing himself. This is nothing to celebrate. Leaders in the Church still fail today. We've all see abusers, hypocrites, cowards, and proud boasters who claim the name of Christ.

But sometimes a leader's failure is not their fault. Before Saul's death, the Philistines killed his three sons, including Jonathan. As the heir to the throne, Jonathan had given the kingdom over to David and served God faithfully. It's one thing to see a leader fall because of their own sin, but it's another to see them fall because of tragedy. How could God let this happen?

Unfortunately, this world is devastatingly broken by sin. The loss of Jonathan (and Saul) was a reminder that Israel needed more than a man to hope in. We too need more than a good pastor, good parents, a good spouse, or a faithful friend. We can't ultimately put our hope in people, no matter how good they are. They are still people. We often criticize or praise leaders in the place of God because they are easier to control, rely upon, or blame. We need to see that while not all leaders end up disgraced in their sin, all fail to live with perfect righteousness and all fail to bring about perfect victory. There's only one who can do that. He is a man and he is also God.

When the Body Fails

But what if more than a leader fails? In 1 Samuel 31, the nation of Israel is defeated. The story is quick, factual, and utterly devastating. In thirteen short verses, words for death are used four times, words for falling or fleeing are used three times each, words for thrust through or striped are used twice each, and there are single mentions of *stuck down, wounded,* and *cut off.* The battle is brutal, and there is no rescue. As the leader fails, so do the people of God. And it gets worse. The land which God created for Israel, called Abraham to, promised to Moses in Egypt, delivered to Joshua, and organized under Saul was now lost. *"The men of Israel... abandoned their cities and fled. And the Philistines came and lived in them"* (31:7). The people had fallen.

The Church knows this feeling all too well. We've regularly failed in our mission to love the nations and our neighbors. Publicly, we've been silent when we should have spoken, and we've spoken when we should have been silent. Most troubling, we've often lost our grip on the gospel. What's the Church to do? For one, we need to be honest about our failures. Likewise, we need to repent by continually turning back to Christ and his Word. Finally, we need to see ourselves as Christ does. He's not surprised by our sin. He's pursued us in it, forgiven us, washed us, and is working tenderly to heal us. He's proved this by dying for us. There is hope for this broken body. Don't let anyone tell you otherwise.

When the World Rejoices

As 1 Samuel ends, the Philistines rejoice by decapitating Saul and sending messengers to spread the "good" news. But it wasn't just the people of God who were being shamed. By desecrating the body of God's anointed man and putting his armor on display in their temple, the Philistines were declaring that God had lost and their gods, Dagon and Ashtaroth, had won.

How do you respond when the world rejoices over the Church's failures? If your concern is your own reputation and pride then you'll either become hateful or you'll defect. But if your concern is the Lord then you'll stay steadfast and do what you can in your grief. *"When the inhabitants of Jabesh-gilead heard what the Philistines had done... all the valiant men arose... and took the (bodies) from the wall... And they took their bones and buried them... and fasted seven days"* (31:12–13). The men of Jabesh-gilead knew that Saul and Israel had failed, and they felt righteous anger that God's name was being shamed. So they quietly did what they could, at the risk of their lives, to honor God.

We've reached the end of 1 Samuel and the picture is bleak. Israel is without a king, prophet, most of their priests, and most of the royal heirs to the throne. Israel has been scattered like sheep without a shepherd. Today's Church is often here with failed leaders, a struggling body, and proud enemies. The Church was also here on a spring day 2,000 years ago when their Leader was killed, lesser leaders failed, and the body scattered as enemies rejoiced. But out of this darkest black, a light came forth: Jesus, risen from the dead, victorious! There is hope for Israel as 1 Samuel concludes and the for Church today. God's chosen Shepherd will lead us to redemption. Indeed, the Church should handle defeat better than anyone else because we're the only ones who can honestly say that our future is secure.

Pause for a Moment

Reflect: How do you handle failure in your life?

Request: Ask God to give you confidence in his victory, in light of your failures.

Respond: The next time you are criticized, make yourself pause. Remember that your value is not based on your performance, your value is from the Lord. Respond in grace.

PART 2

REIGN OF THE KING

After this David inquired of the Lord, "Shall I go up into any of the cities of Judah?" And the Lord said to him, "Go up." David said, "To which shall I go up?" And he said, "To Hebron." So David went up there, and his two wives also, Ahinoam of Jezreel and Abigail the widow of Nabal of Carmel. And David brought up his men who were with him, everyone with his household, and they lived in the towns of Hebron. And the men of Judah came, and there they anointed David king over the house of Judah. When they told David, "It was the men of Jabesh-gilead who buried Saul," David sent messengers to the men of Jabesh-gilead and said to them, "May you be blessed by the Lord, because you showed this loyalty to Saul your lord and buried him. Now may the Lord show steadfast love and faithfulness to you. And I will do good to you because you have done this thing. Now therefore let your hands be strong, and be valiant, for Saul your lord is dead, and the house of Judah has anointed me king over them." But Abner the son of Ner, commander of Saul's army, took Ish-bosheth the son of Saul and brought him over to Mahanaim, and he made him king over Gilead and the Ashurites and Jezreel and Ephraim and Benjamin and all Israel. Ish-bosheth, Saul's son, was forty years old when he began to reign over Israel, and he reigned two years. But the house of Judah followed David. And the time that David was king in Hebron over the house of Judah was seven years and six months.

(2 Samuel 2:1–11)

THE REAL DEAL

(2 Samuel 2:1–11)

As a young man, Frank Abagnale discovered that the average person has a difficult time spotting a counterfeit. Between the ages of fifteen and twenty-one, Abagnale became the most famous con artist in American history. He impersonated a Pan Am Airline pilot and logged over a million miles in flights. He impersonated a sociology professor and taught an entire semester at Brigham Young University. He impersonated a lawyer in Louisiana and served as the Chief Resident Pediatrician at a Georgia hospital. All told, Abagnale fooled thousands of people.[1]

Can you spot a fake? In 2 Samuel 2 we get a glimpse of two different kingdoms. Both have kings, land, and citizens. Can you tell which one is real? In your life are you able to spot the things that honor God as well as the things that don't? It's not an easy task. Counterfeits usually look attractive, they often make us feel good, and they seem logical. Because of this, David reminds God's people that everything depends on choosing the right kingdom. Nothing could be more important. So how does God help us do this?

God-Rooted

If something is really from God, it must originate from him. David's kingdom is no exception. *"And the men of Judah came, and they anointed David king over the house of Judah"* (2:4). As David establishes his kingdom he is anointed, or set apart, for God's purposes with the blessing of God's people.

This moment is significant because it's rooted in the promises of God. Earlier, God's prophet Samuel anointed David, according to God's command, as a preview and guarantee of this day.[2] Before that, David's ancestor Judah was told that God's king would come from his family line.[3] Even before that, David's ancestor Abraham had been given a similar promise.[4] Here, the elders of Judah are simply recognizing what God has been planning all along. This is important. For the first time in the history of the world, God's chosen king visibly reigns on earth according to God's command and promise.[5]

But there's another kingdom being established. *"But Abner... commander of Saul's army, took Ish-bosheth the son of Saul... and he made him king"* (2:8). What are Ish-bosheth's roots? He's a surviving son of Saul. Nevertheless, he hasn't been anointed, the people of God haven't recognized God's calling in his life, no prophet has declared him king, and God has made no promises concerning him. His kingdom is rooted shallowly in man's promises alone.

We can't always see the roots of things, but they make a world of difference. The native buffalo grass of my community in Western Kansas only reaches a maximum height of eight inches, but it can survive our fierce winds and frequent droughts because its roots drop nine feet below the surface.[6] Roots matter. Every book you read, every show you watch, every political idea you hear, every family tradition you practice, and every religious opinion you hold has roots leading back to something. The question is where? Are the roots eternal and secure or are they shallow and shifting?

God-Ruled

If something is really from God, it must also be ruled by him. David knew it was time to become king, but he wanted to make sure that his plans were approved by God. *"David inquired of the LORD, 'Shall I go up into any of the cities of Judah?' And the LORD said, 'Go up.' David said, 'To which shall I go up?' And he said, 'To Hebron.' So David went up. . ."* (2:1–2). David learned in the wilderness that the Kingdom was not his to grab, but rather God's to give. Therefore, David takes direction from God and, trusting his word, brings his men and family to join him in what will come next. He's all in.

On the other hand, Ish-bosheth's kingdom followed a different type of direction. Saul's relative and captain Abner tells Ish-bosheth that he will be king, and he declares it so for all God's people. On the outside it probably made sense to many. After all, Ish-bosheth was a natural heir to the throne. But Abner's actions betray the fact that God is not at work in this kingdom. All the verbs in the passage describe what Abner is doing, not God. Abner takes, he brings, he makes. Both kingdoms are being led, but only one is being led by God.

Don't be deceived. Today, many people claim to be Bible-rooted, but their actions, when studied closely, betray them. We're all capable of twisting God's Word for our purposes. We need to ask ourselves some good questions. Is the Bible making your life more comfortable and convenient? Is it making you more popular and independent of God? If so beware, it sounds like you are ruling. Or is the Bible making your life more difficult, requiring more patience, sacrifice, and dependence upon the Lord? If so, you're probably letting God take the lead.

God-Giving

Finally, if something is really from God it must also be God-giving. As David seeks to establish his kingdom, he shares the grace of God with those he encounters. There's a small story sandwiched between the rise of the two kingdoms. It concerns the town of Jabesh-Gilead and their need to decide which kingdom they will support. David sends a three-part message to them. First, he thanks and blesses them in God's name for risking their lives to give Saul and his sons an honorable burial. Second, David promises, *"I will do good to you because you have done this thing"* (2:6). And finally, instead of threatening them, he invites them to choose the real kingdom.

There's only one right kingdom, and David is graciously inviting the town of Jabesh-Gilead to join it. As we will see in the coming chapters, Ish-bosheth's kingdom will spread nothing good. He will only rule for two years, and his reign will spread death, lies, and disaster. The fruit or resulting output of each kingdom couldn't be any more different.

After counterfeiting and defrauding his way through life, Frank Abagnale was finally arrested and offered a choice. He could stick to his way (or his kingdom) and spend life behind bars. Or, he could work for the FBI and teach them how to spot fakes. Frank accepted the invitation. Like Frank and the men of Jabesh-Gilead we've all been given an invitation. We're surrounded by a kingdom that looks real and feels comfortable. But Jesus offers something else. It will be less comfortable now. It will require submission, sacrifice, and dependence. But it also offers grace. Grace to sincere men like those in Jabesh-Gilead and grace to men like Frank Abagnale who've done everything wrong. Only one kingdom offers this. Will you take part in it?

Pause for a Moment

Reflect: In America, where do Christians need to be especially watchful of spiritual counterfeits?

Request: Ask God for wisdom to see both the roots and the fruit of the influential voices in your life so that you're able to know what is of God and what is not.

Respond: Give grace today. In light of the eternal grace Jesus shared with you, find a small way to be gracious today, especially to someone who doesn't deserve it.

Abner... and the servants of Ish-bosheth... went... to Gibeon. And Joab... and the servants of David... met them... And the battle was very fierce that day. And Abner and the men of Israel were beaten... And the three sons of Zeruiah were there, Joab, Abishai, and Asahel... And Asahel pursued Abner... Therefore Abner struck him... And he fell there and died... There was a long war between the house of Saul and the house of David. And David grew stronger and stronger, while the house of Saul became weaker and weaker. Now Saul had a concubine... And Ish-bosheth said to Abner, "Why have you gone in to my father's concubine?" Then Abner was very angry... and said, "... To this day I keep showing steadfast love to the house of Saul your father... And yet you charge me today with a fault concerning a woman. God do so to Abner and more also, if I do not accomplish for David what the Lord has sworn to him, to transfer the kingdom from the house of Saul and set up the throne of David over Israel and over Judah"... Abner sent messengers to David... saying, "... my hand shall be with you to bring over all Israel to you."... David made a feast for Abner... And Abner said... "I will arise and... gather all Israel to my lord the king..." when Abner returned... Joab took him aside... to speak with him privately, and there he struck him in the stomach, so that he died, for the blood of Asahel his brother... David... said, "I and my kingdom are forever guiltless before the Lord for the blood of Abner... May it fall upon the head of Joab... and may the house of Joab never be without one who has a discharge or who is leprous or who holds a spindle or who falls by the sword or who lacks bread!"
(2 Samuel 2:12–3:29)

EVERYONE HAS FAITH

(2 Samuel 2:12–3:39)

Who has faith? Most Christians wrongly assume that only the religious have faith. Our passage today says otherwise. David has faith that God's way is best. At the same time, General Abner has faith in himself. Both men had faith. The same is true today. Everyone ultimately hopes in something whether it's their politics, success, possessions, knowledge, choice of pleasures, or the "goodness" of humanity. Instead of asking someone *if* they have faith, it's more accurate to ask them *what* they have faith in.

The Bible calls us to put our faith in God. Only He can forgive our sins, make us righteous, and promise us an eternal kingdom. David trusts that this is true. Abner does not. But let's not over simplify it. Every believer, David included, struggles with doubts at times. And when we do, we're tempted to put our faith in things other than God. Let's spend some time examining this problem of misplaced faith:

Our Strength

If God isn't powerful, then isn't it our strength that matters? That's what Abner thought. Trusting in his own military strength, Abner moved the troops of Ish-bosheth, his puppet king, up to the border of David's kingdom thinking that he would win any encounter. Remember, Abner knows what God has promised David. He simply trusts himself more. He initiates a deadly competition between the troops and this leads to a full-out battle. [1] Abner's men are badly defeated. In retreat, Abner kills a man he shouldn't have, and this starts a blood feud with the man's family that will eventually lead to Abner's untimely death. On this day, however, Abner ends up cornered and begging for mercy before he is allowed to flee. Abner's strength fails him.

On the other hand, David, trusting in God's strength, finds success. *"There was a long war between the house of Saul and the house of David. And David grew stronger and stronger, while the house of Saul became weaker and weaker"* (3:1). While Abner trusts in his power and loses it, David trusts in God's and gains it.

Before we look down on Abner we should consider how familiar his temptation is to us. We see it every single day in advertising. Nike tells us to "Just Do It" while Adidas tells us that "Impossible Is Nothing." Gatorade calls us to "Be Like Mike" and Ford dares us to "Go Further." Cadillac encourages us to "Dare Greatly" and Burger King entices us to "Have It [Our] Way." In other words, trust yourself! Believe it or not, this isn't just an American struggle. Every other religion and philosophy in the world tells us that there are things we must and can do through devotion, learning, hard work, sacrifice, or sincerity that will make us right with a god, gods, or the universe itself. The Bible is different. It says that only God can do what is needed. All we can do is take our need to him. Whose strength will you trust? It makes an eternal difference.

Our Authority

If God isn't in charge, then isn't it us who decide what is right? Abner thought so. He proved this by making two power plays in Ish-bosheth's kingdom. First, Abner decided that it was permissible for him to sleep with the former king's concubine (it wasn't). To do so was to claim the king's "property"[2] and make a bid for the throne. It was a gutsy move, and King Ish-bosheth called him out on it.

Instead of realizing his sin, Abner is outraged that someone would question his authority and integrity. In response he attempts an even bigger power play, telling the king, "*God do so to Abner and more also, if I do not accomplish for David what the LORD has sworn to him, to transfer the kingdom from the house of Saul and set up the throne of David over Israel and over Judah*" (3:9–10). If Abner couldn't get what he wanted with Ish-bosheth, he'd get it with David. Notice his pious God-talk as if he was really concerned about God's authority. It's clear he wasn't. Abner could talk the religious talk, but at the end of the day Abner did what Abner wanted to do. In his mind, he was the only authority worth consulting. Do you ever use God talk to mask your desire for authority? In time, it will become clear which authority we trust.

Our Control

If God isn't in control, then aren't we able to be? Abner shouted amen to this. Putting all his ducks in order, Abner made peace with David over a meal, returned David's first wife to him upon his request,[3] and convinced the elders of Israel to unite the nations. Everything was working perfectly for Abner. He was in control as the master puppeteer. But not for long.

Here's what happened: *"And when Abner returned to Hebron, Joab took him aside into the midst of the gate to speak with him privately, and there he struck him in the stomach, so that he died, for the blood of Asahel his brother"* (3:27). Just like that, Abner's schemes, control, and life were over. Gone in a moment of betrayal and murder.

Sadly, as one Abner dies, we're introduced to another: David's general Joab. Thinking that he could exert control over his life, Joab used his strength, with only his own approval, to end an illegal blood feud and make sure that Abner didn't challenge his place in David's army. Joab did all this even though it meant committing an act of treason, breaking the peace, and sinfully killing another man in cold blood. But Joab wasn't in control either. He was publicly rebuked, forced to grieve for the man he killed, and rightly cursed by King David. There is a cost for playing God. Both Joab and Abner learned this the hard way.

The scariest thing about Abner and Joab is the fact that the Church is filled with thousands of them today. Countless men and women foolishly trust their own strength, authority, and control while falsely claiming God's approval. Even scarier is the fact that every believer feels this tug of Abner and Joab upon their heart daily. But we are not without hope. Even with Abner and Joab running amok, God establishes his Kingdom through David and has done the same with his Son. Jesus proves this by loving his Joab-like disciples and dying for them. He continues to prove this by loving his Joab-like

Church and leading her by grace daily so that we can say, with repentant hearts "Your kingdom come, your will be done."[4]

Pause for a Moment

Reflect: In what ways do you trust your own strength, authority, and control like Abner and Joab?

Request: Ask God to reveal the plans in your life that do not fit his Kingdom. Ask him to soften your grip and help you let go.

Respond: Identify situations in your life that are beyond your strength, authority, and control. Thank God for these and ask him how you might serve him well in them.

When Ish-bosheth, Saul's son, heard that Abner had died. . . his courage failed, and all Israel was dismayed. Now Saul's son had two men who were captains of raiding bands; the name of the one was Baanah, and the name of the other Rechab, sons of Rimmon a man of Benjamin. . . Now. . . Rechab and Baanah, set out, and. . . came to the house of Ish-bosheth as he was taking his noonday rest. And they came into the midst of the house as if to get wheat, and they stabbed him in the stomach. Then Rechab and Baanah his brother escaped. When they came into the house, as he lay on his bed. . . they struck him and put him to death and beheaded him. They took his head and went by the way of the Arabah all night, and brought the head of Ish-Bosheth. . . to David at Hebron. And they said to the king, "Here is the head of Ish-bosheth, the son of Saul, your enemy, who sought your life. The LORD has avenged my lord the king this day on Saul and on his offspring." But David answered. . . "As the LORD lives, who has redeemed my life out of every adversity, when one told me, 'Behold, Saul is dead,' and thought he was bringing good news, I seized him and killed him. . . which was the reward I gave him for his news. How much more, when wicked men have killed a righteous man in his own house on his bed, shall I not now require his blood at your hand and destroy you from the earth?" And David commanded his young men, and they killed them and cut off their hands and feet and hanged them beside the pool at Hebron. But they took the head of Ish-bosheth and buried it in the tomb of Abner at Hebron.

(2 Samuel 4)

LOOKING AT THE HEART

(2 Samuel 4)

It was the last play of the game. The score was tied. As quarterback, it was my job to secure the win. There was just one problem. My best receiver was four-foot six and Shawn, the other team's five-foot five giant, was guarding him. This was fourth-grade recess, and I may or may not have been jealous of this Shawn kid. Back to the story. I took the snap, threw deep, and Shawn, of course, swooped in, picked off the pass, and began running it back to win the game. I was the last guy left, but he was faster. I had to stop him. We play to win, right? So, I cheated. I tripped Shawn from behind, and the gamed ended as a tie.

Was that ok? Did the ends (saving the game) justify the means (cheating)? As long as you accomplish a good goal, aren't you free to do it however you wish? Do you ever get tempted like this? To cut corners to get a job done or to tell a white lie to make a situation easier? What if it just takes a tiny little sin to do something really good? This is what we find in 2 Samuel 4. Two men accomplish their reasonable goals with shady work. Is it acceptable? Absolutely not. God cares about our hearts. Sinful motives are never acceptable no matter what good goal they accomplish. "For the LORD sees not as man sees: man looks on the outward appearance, but the LORD looks on the heart."[1] God cares about your heart. We must do the right things for the right reasons. How do we make sure to do this?

Resisting the World's Ways

If we're not aware of the world's influence upon us, we'll end up acting like it. Our story introduces us to two men, Baanah and Rechab, who are very much products of the world. The biblical author gives us hints about this so that we know what to expect. Both men are from the tribe of Benjamin. This was Saul's tribe, and he had been an ungodly ruler. Both men also worked for Ish-bosheth, Saul's son and another man who lived according to the world. Finally, their names are introduced to us in the middle of several unfortunate events.[2] Beware, the writer is telling us, something is off with these men.

Here's the thing. These men are worldly, but they're not idiots. They serve Ish-bosheth who is ruling in the North, but they can read the writing on the wall. They know they're on the losing side. They only have a few options.

First, they could stay with Ish-bosheth, but this would probably result in them dying in battle. Second, they could surrender to David, but this would probably result in them becoming prisoners and losing their power. Finally, they could find a way to switch sides while keeping their power. They picked the final option. "*Now... Rechab and Baanah... came to the house of Ish-bosheth as he was taking his noonday rest... they struck him and... took his head and went by the way of the Arabah all night*" (4:5–7). The plan goes smoothly, but we're not supposed to be impressed.[3] The biblical author wants to emphasize that they were so "brave" that they killed their own king while he was sleeping in bed and then ran away as fast as they could. Really "brave." Really worldly. Really wrong.

But are we really that different when we make plans? We often ask: Will this work? Will this get the job done? Or will this help us? Sadly, we forget to ask: Is this right? What are my motives? Or does this reflect Jesus' heart? Better questions are a good place to start!

Embracing God's Ways

To embrace God's ways, we have to first know them. Listen to the way that Rechab and Baanah interpret their actions, *"They said to [David], 'Here is the head of Ish-bosheth... your enemy, who sought your life. The LORD avenged my lord the king this day...'"* (4:8). Rechab and Baanah use God-talk to excuse their actions: "They come with blood on their hands but theology on their lips."[4] How often this happens among God's people! But is this the way God really works? Of course not and David knows it. *"But David answered... 'As the LORD lives who has redeemed my life out of every adversity....'"* (4:9). We'll finish that sentence in a moment. Stop and enjoy the *but* here. These guys know how to talk theology, *but* David knows the Lord. And this doesn't match up. You can't embrace God's ways without knowing him.

Because he knows God, David knows who he must praise and who he must not. Taking a formal vow, David distances himself from these men noting that God alone has saved him from trouble. David doesn't need dirty henchmen. He needs God. *"When one told me, 'Behold, Saul is dead,' and thought he was bringing good news, I seized him and killed him... How much more, when wicked men have killed a righteous man in his own house... shall I not now require his blood at your hand and destroy you from this earth?"* (4:10–11). We didn't cover the story about Saul's messenger, but it's the same thing that happens here. When someone boasts in doing evil in the name of good, they deserve justice not praise.

So... do the ends justify the means? I learned that lesson the hard way back in fourth grade. As I went to trip Shawn our feet got tangled. I did "save" the game, but I also landed awkwardly and broke my arm. Embarrassing. Whether we see it now or later, there are always consequences for embracing the ways of the world.

Learning this the hard way, Rechab and Baanah were put to death by David. Was this appropriate? Remember who David is. He's God's king who has been given divine authority to execute justice in Israel. This means punishing the wicked *and* giving justice to the oppressed (a gracious burial is given to Ish-bosheth). This was David's job because David points to a greater king, Jesus, whose justice has a much greater reach. Praise God that the blood of Jesus makes us his friends so that we too are not judged but forgiven. Praise God that Jesus will do what is right and good by dealing justly with those who murder, steal, hate, abuse the Church, and spread the evils of genocide, infanticide, and racism, all without repentance. Praise God that relief and justice will come to all who suffer and trust in him. Our God always does the right thing for the right reason. May we do the same.

Pause for a Moment

Reflect: When was the last time you were tempted to do something "good" for the wrong reasons?

Request: Ask God to make your heart more and more like His on a daily basis.

Respond: Next time you serve others, ask good questions about your motives and trust in Jesus' grace to both forgive and empower you.

Then all the tribes of Israel came to David. . . and said, "Behold, we are your bone and flesh. . . the LORD said to you, 'You shall be shepherd of my people Israel. . .'" So. . . King David made a covenant with them. . . before the LORD, and they anointed David king over Israel. . . And the king and his men went to Jerusalem against the Jebusites. . . who said to David, "You will not come in here, but the blind and the lame will ward you off"—thinking, "David cannot come in here." Nevertheless, David took the stronghold of Zion, that is, the city of David. And David said on that day, "Whoever would strike the Jebusites, let him get up the water shaft to attack 'the lame and the blind,'. . . And David became greater and greater, for the LORD, the God of hosts, was with him. And Hiram king of Tyre sent messengers to David, and cedar trees, also carpenters and masons who built David a house. And David knew that the LORD had established him. . . and. . . exalted his kingdom for the sake of his people Israel. . . the Philistines went up to search for David. But David. . . inquired of the LORD, "Shall I go up against the Philistines?". . . the LORD said. . . "Go up, for I will certainly give the Philistines into your hand." And. . . David defeated them. . . And he said, "The LORD has broken through my enemies. . . like a breaking flood.". . . And the Philistines came up yet again. . . And when David inquired of the LORD, he said, "You shall not go up; go around. . . And when you hear the sound of marching in the tops of the balsam trees, then rouse yourself, for then the LORD has gone out before you to strike down the army of the Philistines." And David did as the LORD commanded him, and struck down the Philistines from Geba to Gezer.

(2 Samuel 5)

HOPE FOR THE WORLD

(2 Samuel 5)

Isn't it easy to look at the news and lose hope for where our country and world are heading? Disasters, poverty, violence, injustice, and economic uncertainty are just a few of the things we regularly hear about. We have plenty of reasons to question the trajectory of our world. Is there any hope? The easy answer would be no. And even if we admit that there is hope, most Christians act and talk like there's not. But Scripture refuses to let us stay in this place. In fact, the story of the Bible is the story of a God who, knowing our brokenness and sin better than we do, promises and works to make everything right. And God always keeps his promises. So what should we specifically be hoping for?

A Leader

The darker the times the more desperate we become for leadership. Israel was no exception. They needed God to unite them. And he did, *"Then all the tribes of Israel came to David. . . and said, "Behold, we are your bone and flesh. . . the* LORD *said to you, 'You shall be shepherd of my people Israel. . .' So. . . King*

David made a covenant with them. . .' " (5:1–3). Israel needed a leader who was like them and right with God. By God's gracious plan, David was both of these things.

We've mentioned it before, but it's worth remembering that in making David king of Israel God was keeping at least five promises. God had promised fallen Eve that a human leader would rise up from her broken family.[1] He promised Abraham that kings would descend from him.[2] He promised Moses that he would choose a king in the future.[3] After Saul failed, God promised a king after his own heart. God keeps his word. David was an answered promise worth celebrating. We too must pray for good leadership. Even so, David was imperfect[4] and couldn't ultimately save Israel. Therefore, we must be careful to rest our hope for a leader upon the Greater David, Jesus.

A Land

One of the reasons why we hope for leaders is so that we can live free and flourishing lives with the people that God has given us. And for this to happen, we need a home. We need a land. David's next step was finding a way to provide this by uniting Judah in the South with Israel in the North. The answer was found in Jerusalem, a small yet strategic city located between the two nations.

The only problem was that Jerusalem was occupied by an enemy nation, the Jebusites, and they knew that God's people had never been able to breach their stronghold, *"'You will not come in here, but the blind and the lame will ward you off'- thinking, 'David cannot come in here' "* (5:6). Trash talk is fun until you have to eat it. David shoves their trash talk back into their face[5] and takes the city with a secret attack. In the coming days even the surrounding nations will confess that God has given his people a united land (5:11).

This particular piece of real estate had a history. When Abraham was promised a land for his descendants, the land of the Jebusites was included in the list.[6] The only problem was that Israel had failed to take this city for 800 years. But now, God's Word had come true, *"David knew that the* LORD *had established him king over Israel, and that he had exalted his kingdom for the sake of his people Israel"* (5:12). Old promises are not invalid promises when it comes to God.

Do you have a place that carries great significance such as a childhood home, your favorite stretch of land, or a cabin in the woods? My grandparent's country property, "The Farm," was that place for me. It was strategically located away from my family's busy suburban life. I remember burnt hot dogs, mossy fishing adventures, life lessons learned while sitting on a tailgate, and coyote howls in the darkness.

Christians tend to forget that we are both spiritual *and* physical creatures designed to connect with places. We need places to raise our kids, to laugh with friends, to grow our food, to exercise, to learn, to work, and to worship. Creation was made for this. Like Israel, we yearn for these places to be safe from violence, for our homes to be sound, for our land to be fruitful, and for the weather to be helpful.

Thankfully, we have a twofold hope in this. First, God promises to join us in our work as we pursue the good of our community and land even now as faithful stewards. Second, we know that later we will see this work finished by God in the new heavens *and* the new earth that he promises to share with all his people.[7] Even on the other side of eternity, this hope for a good land will be experienced and enjoyed.

A Victory

Sadly, David's throne and Israel's land are quickly in danger as the Philistines attack again. In this broken world, it often feels like we never get a break. But our God is a protector, and he provides David with victory. Twice before major battles David stops and asks God for help. Once, God tells David to fight right away and once God tells David to wait. This is not a formulaic relationship with God, but rather one of dependence and trust. Both times Israel wins, the Philistines run, and the nation is secure. All David can do is praise the One who provided the victory, *"The LORD has broken through my enemies before me like a breaking flood"* (5:20). David knows that God's patience and plan are not a sign of weakness. God keeps his promises, and *He* secures the victory.

God's promise of a leader, a land, and an ultimate victory should make Christians the most optimistic people in the world. The trick, however, is putting our optimism in the right things. Not ourselves, not our political party, not our success, not our nation, nor even the degree to which we influence our culture. Rather, our optimism is in the spread of the Kingdom under the leadership of our greater David, King Jesus. Jesus was one of us, but he was also more than us. Right with the Father, he was rejected by the leaders of world and hung on a cross, in a desolate spot, in apparent defeat. But God keeps his word, and King Jesus smashed the enemies of sin, Satan, and death as he rose victorious. This is where our confidence stems from, and this is our hope for all that is *yet* to come. May we wait with confidence!

Pause for a Moment

Reflect: As a Christian, have you been tempted to forget that God cares about both the physical and the spiritual? Which one have you most neglected?

Request: Pray for your leaders, the good of your community and land, and the advance of God's kingdom.

Respond: Take note of the first time you feel fear today. Remind yourself that your God is the smasher of all wicked and evil things. Rest in him.

And David... went... to bring up... the ark of God... And they carried the ark... on a new cart... And David and all the house of Israel were celebrating before the LORD, with songs and lyres... and cymbals... Uzzah put out his hand to the ark of God and took hold of it, for the oxen stumbled. And the anger of the LORD was kindled against Uzzah, and God struck him down.... because of his error, and he died... David was angry because the LORD had broken out against Uzzah...And David was afraid... So David was not willing to take the ark... into the city of David. But David took it aside to the house of Obed-edom... and the LORD blessed Obed-edom and all his household... So David went and brought up the ark... to the city of David with rejoicing. And when those who bore the ark... had gone six steps, he sacrificed an ox and a fattened animal. And David danced before the LORD with all his might And David was wearing a... ephod... Michal the daughter of Saul... saw King David leaping and dancing before the LORD, and she despised him in her heart... And when David had finished offering the burnt offerings and the peace offerings, he blessed the people in the name of the LORD of hosts and distributed among all the people... a cake of bread, a portion of meat... to each... But Michal... said, "How the king of Israel honored himself today, uncovering himself... before the eyes of his... female servants, as one of the vulgar fellows..."And David said... "It was before the LORD, who chose me above your father... to appoint me as prince over Israel... and I will celebrate before the LORD. I will make myself yet more contemptible than this, and I will be abased in your eyes. But by the female servants... I shall be held in honor." And Michal... had no child to the day of her death.

(2 Samuel 6:2–23)

WHAT'S GOD REALLY LIKE?

(2 Samuel 6)

What's God really like? Some people emphasize the power and holiness of God. Taken in isolation, this view can make God into a cruel heavenly boss who demands obedience but gives no grace. Others emphasize the love and grace of God. Taken in isolation, this view can make God into a laid-back buddy who isn't overly concerned with anything other than sappy sentiment. Obviously, neither extreme is satisfying. To be fair, the Bible sympathizes with this struggle to describe God. It tells us that "there is no one holy like the LORD"[1] and that "[God's] love is better than life!"[2] Today, David and Israel will learn, with both joy and pain, that both of these realities are simultaneously true. There is no one as holy as our God, and there is no one as loving as our God. So how do we interact with a God like this?

Respecting Holiness

Here's the situation. David is reigning as Israel's victorious king in the capital city of Jerusalem, but he's missing one thing: the ark. Why is this important? This small gold-covered wooden box was no magic weapon, though it was powerful,[3] but rather the tangible symbol of God's special presence with his people. Whenever it was carried forth, the priests would announce, "Arise, O LORD" and then "Return, O LORD" when they halted.[4] Encapsulated inside were various symbols of God's presence including the Ten Commandments. It was only fitting therefore that this sign of God's presence and power be the center of David's new kingdom.

While God's holy presence in the ark was a blessing, it was also dangerous. Israel had been given three specific warnings about this. They were not to touch the ark, look into it, or move it with anything other than poles.[5] They didn't listen. Putting the ark on an oxen cart, David organized a giant moving party before this happened, "*Uzzah put out his hand to the ark of God and took hold of it for the oxen stumbled. And the anger of the LORD was kindled against Uzzah, and God struck him down...*" (6:6–7). With the best of intentions, Uzzah reaches out to keep the ark from falling off the cart and, in touching the unique symbol of God's holy presence as a mere man, he is struck down and dies. The party is over. David is frustrated and angry, but there's nothing that can be done. The ark is left behind and everyone, except Uzzah, goes home.

Have you ever seen a killer whale up close? With striking black and white coloration, up to four tons of weight, thirty-two feet of length, and four-inch teeth these are indeed magnificent animals. Even more amazing is the fact that there are zero recorded incidents of these massive creatures ever killing a human in the wild.[6] It appears that when these animals are encountered on their own terms they are surprisingly safe. However, as people have captured these animals and tried to interact with them on our own terms, in aquariums that is, the statistics have changed. In confined tanks and with constant human contact, there have been numerous killer whale attacks on humans including multiple fatalities.[7] What accounts for the difference? Respect. Approaching a mighty and magnificent creature on our own terms is always foolish.

The same is true of our God. He is mighty, fierce, and awesome. He is not a fuzzy friend in the sky, and he will not be treated that way. He is to be respected by all. Ignoring His Word and disregarding His ways is neither safe nor good for you. This must influence the way we speak, worship, make decisions, and live.

Enjoying Grace

While God is always holy and never ceases to be, holiness alone does not adequately describe Him. God's judgment is never the last word for his people. Indeed, the true intention of the ark was to bless the people of God, not destroy them. Obed-edom, the poor man left to "watch over" over the ark, is immensely blessed by it. Realizing his error and seeing God's blessing on Obed-edom, David returns for the ark and *"Danced before the LORD with all his might. And David was wearing a[n]... ephod"* (6:12–14) The problem wasn't that David lacked joy the first time, but rather that he had celebrated without obeying.

This time David obeys and celebrates, dancing with all his might. As he enters Jerusalem, David comes as both a leader who provides for his people and a priest (his choice of clothing, the ephod, reflects this) who leads worship. This type of celebrating can only happen when we see the goodness of God in light of our brokenness.

But is it really possible to behave like this before a holy God? It depends on what you know. David's wife Michal didn't approve: *"she despised him in her heart"* (6:16). In Michal's eyes, David had humiliated himself as a fool instead of acting like a dignified King. David's response didn't mince words. *"It was before the LORD, who chose me above your father... to appoint me as prince over Israel... and I will celebrate before the LORD. I will make myself yet more contemptible than this, and I will be abased in your eyes"* (6:21–22). Unlike Michal's father Saul who used God to get worship, David will lead the nation by genuinely worshipping God. He's not out to impress anyone other than God, and nothing could be more regal.

Let's be blunt. It would be a lot easier to understand a simple God: one who was only gracious, but not holy or only holy, but not gracious. But this wouldn't be the real God. This would make him unapproachable or unjust. And it would also let us off the hook of needing a relationship with this good, yet complex God.

Instead, the only way to have a relationship with this God is to know him as he reveals himself to us in the person of Jesus Christ, the greater King David. Those who say God can't be all holy and all good at the same time haven't met this God-man. Like David, Jesus united the roles of priest and king by bringing the presence of God to the people of God. Jesus, however, brought this presence by bringing himself. Only in Jesus is God's presence safe for us because it has been covered by the blood he offered on the cross. He is the one we come to trembling with joy and of whom we "delight in the fear of."[8] In Jesus, the righteous holiness of God is satisfied so that his grace might be applied to all who seek it.

Pause for a Moment

Reflect: Are you more tempted to see God as a tense boss or a laid-back buddy?

Request: Ask God to use his Word to help you more accurately understand and relate to him as both holy and gracious. He promises to answer this request.

Respond: Think about how your view of God affects the way you share Him with others. Today, speak of God and walk with Him in a balanced way.

Now when... the LORD had given him rest from all his...
enemies, the king said to Nathan the prophet, "See now, I
dwell in a house of cedar, but the ark of God dwells in a
tent"... The word of the LORD came to Nathan, "... Would you
build me a house to dwell in?... In all places where I have
moved... did I speak a word... saying, "Why have you not built
me a house of cedar?.... Thus says the LORD... I took you from
the pasture... that you should be prince... And I have been
with you wherever you went... And I will make for you a great
name... And I will appoint a place for my people Israel... And
I will give you rest from all your enemies... the LORD will make
you a house. When your days are fulfilled... I will raise up your
offspring after you... and I will establish his kingdom. He shall
build a house for my name, and I will establish the throne of
his kingdom forever. I will be to him a father, and he shall be
to me a son... my steadfast love will not depart from him...
And your house and your kingdom shall be made sure forever
before me"... Then King David... sat before the LORD and said,
"Who am I, O LORD GOD, and what is my house, that you have
brought me thus far?... Because of your promise, and
according to your own heart, you have brought about all
this... Therefore you are great, O LORD God. For there is none
like you... And who is like your people... the one nation...
whom God went to redeem to be his people, making himself a
name and doing for them great... things by driving out before
your people, whom you redeemed for yourself from Egypt, a
nation and its gods?"
(2 Samuel 7)

18

THE COVENANT

(2 Samuel 7)

Mr. Grant was shivering as he walked through the rain with his umbrella. However, when he spotted a stranger getting soaked, he stopped and invited the man to join him. He simply wanted to help. Most of us like being helpful even when it's slightly inconvenient. It's the right thing to do, and it's often rewarding. As Christians, this often carries over into our relationship with God. We love helping Him. We instinctively see our prayers, acts of service, and generosity as things that we do to help God. The Bible agrees that it's good to serve God.

In this passage, David picks up on that train of thought. God has done so much for him; the least he can do is help God back a little bit. He decides that God's ark needs more than a tent. It needs a house. But herein lies the problem. Subtly, David's desire to serve God shifts into the idea that God *needs* his help. The actions might look the same, but the heart is different. One functions out of worship, the other functions out of pride. David assumes that God needs him to build this house—that he has something that God doesn't. But of course God isn't needy. So how do we make sure our obedience is rooted in worship and not pride?

Trusting God to Care for Himself

Even if we never say it, it's easy to assume that God needs us. David did: *"the king said to Nathan the prophet, 'see now, I dwell in a house of cedar, but the ark of God dwells in a tent' "* (7:2). Can you see the warning signs? David refers to God distantly, as an "it," the *ark of God*. His heart is moving in the direction of helping an "it," not serving his almighty Lord.

God responds by asking David if He's ever lived in a house or asked for one. He wants to know if David thinks he needs one. This is a gentle but firm reminder: Don't mistake my humility for weakness as if a mortal man could provide something for the creator of the universe. Get the picture?

When this sinks in, we're able to see God's greatness. And this brings humility. *"Then King David went in and sat before the LORD and said, 'Who am I, O LORD GOD, and what is my House, that you have brought me thus far? . . . Therefore you are great, O LORD God. For there is none like you. . .'"* (7:18 & 22). Lesson learned, David humbly sits in a posture of worship before the Lord and speaks differently. He's no longer talking to an "it" that needs help, he's talking to a God who is fully self-sufficient.

Trusting God to Care for Us

In the ancient world there was a formula for earning the help of the "gods." A king would build a temple for a god and then he could expect to receive great blessings.[1] Was David guilty of thinking along these lines? The thought probably crossed his mind.

We all want God's help, and we're tempted to think that we can earn it. But that's not how our God works. God gives

David a history lesson. "*I took you from the pasture. . . that you should be prince over my people. . . And I have been with you wherever you went. . . And I will make for you a great name. . .*" (7:8–9). God is reminding David that all of his help has been a free gift. David gets it, "*[We] are the one nation on earth whom God went to redeem to be his people, making himself a name and doing for them great and awesome things by driving out before you people. . . a nation [Egypt] and its gods?*" (7:23). David remembers that God saved his people simply because he loved them. Every other "god" in the world says "give, give, give." David's God is the only one who has kept saying "receive, receive, receive." We must trust that God's provision is gracious, not earned.

Trusting God to Care for the Future

Our fears about the future often push us into "helping mode" with God. We need to remember that God always keeps his promises, including those for the future. This truth is beautifully on display as we turn to one of the most important passages in the Bible, the Davidic Covenant, which is God's promise that David's offspring will have an eternal kingdom.

Listen to this incredible promise: "*. . . The LORD will make you a house. When your days are fulfilled. . . I will raise up your offspring after you. . . and I will establish his kingdom. He shall build a house for my name, and I will establish the throne of his kingdom forever. I will be to him a father, and he shall be to me a son. . . my steadfast love will not depart from him. . . And your house and your kingdom shall be made sure forever before me.*" (7:11–16). Do you see how God has graciously flipped David's offer to build him a temporary house into an offer to build

David an eternal dynasty? And this dynasty will be led by David's descendants who will have an everlasting relationship with God in which God will faithfully keep them despite their brokenness. David leaves this interaction awed by God's provision, asking only that God would make it all so.

Ulysses S. Grant, the eighteenth president of the United States and victorious Civil War general, was walking through the rain with his umbrella when he decided to stop for a wet stranger. Not recognizing President Grant, the stranger made small talk about how awful the current President was. Despite this most inappropriate and shocking insult from someone he was helping, President Grant continued holding the umbrella for the man and kindly walked him to his destination.[2]

In many ways the Davidic Covenant functions like this. The covenant God will not stop walking with David's line even when they fall into grave and shocking sin. Instead, he will see to it that they are redeemed. This promise has proven true. Today, David's name is known throughout the world because of the one particular descendant who fulfilled the promise 2,000 years ago not by making God a new temple, but by being the very temple and presence of God as Jesus, Immanuel, God with us. Today, this particular descendant of David is still on the throne, having conquered sin and death by rising from the dead. Like David, we too can ask with confidence that God would fulfill his promise by returning King Jesus physically to defeat his enemies, provide healing for his people, and finally and fully establish his Kingdom. While God graciously invites us to serve him, we must remember and rejoice that all of his promises find their completion in the second David.

Pause for a Moment

Reflect: In what ways do you find yourself trying to help God?

Request: Ask God to remind you of every promise that he has given you in Jesus.

Respond: Rest easy that God's kingdom does not depend on you. Go and serve him today with the peace and joy of knowing that your service is worship, not help!

David defeated the Philistines and subdued them... And he defeated Moab and... measured them with a line, making them lie down on the ground. Two lines he measured to be put to death, and one full line to be spared. And the Moabites became servants to David and brought tribute. David also defeated Hadadezer... King of Zobah, as he went to restore his power at the river Euphrates. And David took from him 1,700 horsemen, and 20,000 foot soldiers. And David hamstrung all the chariot horses but left enough for 100 chariots. And when the Syrians of Damascus came to help Hadadezer king of Zobah, David struck down 22,000 men of the Syrians. Then David put garrisons in Aram of Damascus, and the Syrians became servants to David... And the LORD gave victory to David wherever he went. And David took the shields of gold that were carried by the servants of Hadadezer and brought them to Jerusalem... When Toi king of Hamath heard that David had defeated the whole army of Hadadezer, Toi sent his son Joram to King David, to ask about his health and to bless him... for Hadadezer had often been at war with Toi. And Joram brought with him articles of silver, of gold, and of bronze. These also King David dedicated to the LORD, together with the silver and gold that he dedicated from all the nations he subdued, from Edom, Moab, the Ammonites, the Philistines, Amalek, and from the spoil of Hadadezer... And David made a name for himself when he returned from striking down 18,000 Edomites in the Valley of Salt... and all the Edomites became David's servants. And the LORD gave victory to David wherever he went. So David reigned over all Israel. And David administered justice and equity to all his people.

(2 Samuel 8:1–14)

19

HISTORY MATTERS

(2 Samuel 8)

Every so often, a bizarre fad sweeps through the nation and we're left asking why. Are you old enough to have owned a pet rock? What about shake weights, pump-up basketball shoes, or spinners? The marketers really got us with those. I'm no exception. I've been had by several trends including, to my great embarrassment, once buying a pair of skinny jeans. They were worn once. Looking back on it all, it's easy to wonder if it really happened. We wish it didn't.

As the people of God read 2 Samuel 8 hundreds of years later, listening to David's victories and reign of justice, they probably found themselves asking a similar question but hoping for the opposite answer. Did it really happen? They hoped that it had. Their current situation was quite different. They were a weak nation with strong enemies, corrupted kings, suffering from exile and destruction. Were things ever that good? Christians today ask similar questions about Jesus and the early Church.[1] We hear of miracles, growth, and radical transformation and we compare it to decline and lukewarm faith. In our discouragement we wonder, did it really happen? We struggle to reconcile what was and what now seems to be.

Thankfully, the Bible is clear that the kingdom really has come. Like a scrapbook picture that confirms your purchase of bell-bottom jeans, this passage confirms that God really has established his kingdom on earth through David. Likewise, through the second David, Jesus, we are reminded that the kingdom is still here and advancing towards its full and final reign. But if the kingdom is hard to see, what should we be looking for to remind us of its presence?

Kingdom Conflict

The kingdom always brings conflict because the kingdom is always resisted. Israel watched their enemies resist God by destroying Israel's crops, kidnapping their children, killing their men, and abusing their women. The same was true in the New Testament when the religious leaders resisted Jesus' grace and put him to death. Just because God's kingdom is here doesn't mean that everyone is willing to accept it

Nevertheless, God is in the business of reclaiming what belongs to him. In David's day this meant battles and victory. David subdued the Philistines, wiped out two-thirds of the Moabite forces, and took down 60,000 troops from the surrounding nations.[2] How? *"The LORD gave victory to David wherever he went"* (8:6 & 14). Through David, God is reclaiming what is rightfully his. Did not Jesus defeat powerful forces of demons, sin, and death itself to reclaim the precious children of the kingdom?

We do need to be careful here. When it comes to kingdom conflict, we better make sure that we are following God's lead. Some of us are too eager for conflict and insist on fighting battles that God doesn't support. These sorts of folks love to stir up conflict on social media, degrade their opponents, and elevate their own status. Sadly, they will in time realize that God is not standing beside them to secure victory.

On the other hand, many modern Christians are embarrassed of conflict, feeling that they are too sophisticated to stir the pot. Have we forgotten the fight that William Wilberforce brought against slavery, the fight that Martin Luther brought against works-based righteousness, or the fight that Mother Teresa brought against the caste system? As another pastor puts it, "The church [today] tends to mute this virile biblical note and thereby emasculates the doctrine of the kingdom... As if people would only be nice enough the kingdom would arrive."[3] There must be conflict, but it must be the right conflict, waged the right way. Yes, one day Jesus will forcefully and violently defeat all of his (and our) enemies. But until then, Jesus teaches us to trust his future victory by fighting with the weapons of the Spirit including prayer, spiritual gifts, and evangelism. Because of this, we do not seek to take life, as warriors of other religions do, but give it, even if it means sacrificing our own for the sake of others.

Kingdom Peace

Ultimately, kingdom conflict leads to kingdom peace because the kingdom is open to all. Notice that David does not strike every nation down. *"When Toi king of Hamath heard that David had defeated the whole army of Hadadezer, Toi sent his son Joram to King David, to ask about his health and to bless him... for Hadadezer had often been at war with Toi. And Joram brought with him articles of silver, of gold, and of bronze"* (8:9–10). This foreign king rejoices in David's victory over a common foe and sends his son with blessings and pledged support.

While some reject the spreading of the kingdom, others will accept it and rejoice. Just as there are Judas' and Pharisees, so too will there be Pauls' and Zacchaeuses'. This is a picture of the future kingdom where "the foreigners who join themselves to the LORD. . . [will be brought to his] holy mountain and [made] joyful. . . Their [offerings] will be accepted. . . For [his] house shall be called a house of prayer for all peoples."[4] The kingdom is truly open to all who would enter. And it's good: *"So David reigned over all Israel. And David administered justice and equity to all his people"* (8:15). Again, Jesus fulfills this picture as he helped the needy, established true justice, and provided eternal security against the attacks of the enemy.

There was a Kansas native who ended up retiring in Mississippi. She was happy to be near family but missed the scenes of her childhood state (as do all who leave the great land of Kansas!). After sharing this with her husband, he decided to bring a taste of Kansas back to their swampy Mississippi home. He planted sunflowers in the backyard, filled one section of the yard with prairie grass, and set up an old windmill. Now, though she no longer lives in Kansas, this woman is able to step out her back door and get a taste of home.[5]

As we've examined the kingdom today we know that one day all conflict will cease and then kingdom peace will reign supreme. But how can we remember this in such a broken world? By following this woman's example. By bringing a taste of the kingdom to the places of this world that we've been called. As we live, work, and play we must intentionally seek to keep the kingdom doors wide open, praying that others, like Toi, may see the goodness of the king and join in. Our enemies are suffering, and they need the healing and peace of our King before it's too late. Serve your family, neighbors, and community, work honestly, share with those in need, and speak the truth about Jesus even when it's difficult. By doing so, we spread the goodness of the kingdom wherever we go. It's just a taste. But through Jesus, more is coming.

Pause for a Moment

Reflect: Is it easier for you to seek kingdom conflict or kingdom peace? Why?

Request: Ask God to humble you when you are too eager for conflict and to embolden you when you are too fearful.

Respond: Share a little taste of the kingdom with someone else today.

And David said, "Is there still anyone left of the house of Saul, that I may show him kindness for Jonathan's sake?". . . Ziba said to the king, "There is still a son of Jonathan; he is crippled in his feet." The king said to him, "Where is he?" And Ziba said to the king, "He is. . .at Lo-debar." Then King David sent and brought him from. . . Lo-debar. And Mephibosheth the son of Jonathan, son of Saul, came to David and fell on his face and paid homage. And David said, "Mephibosheth!" And he answered, "Behold, I am your servant." And David said to him, "Do not fear, for I will show you kindness for the sake of your father Jonathan, and I will restore to you all the land of Saul your father, and you shall eat at my table always." And he paid homage and said, "What is your servant, that you should show regard for a dead dog such as I?" Then the king called Ziba, Saul's servant, and said to him, "All that belonged to Saul and to all his house I have given to your master's grandson. And you and your sons and your servants shall till the land for him and shall bring in the produce, that your master's grandson may have bread to eat. But Mephibosheth. . . shall always eat at my table". . . Then Ziba said to the king, "According to all that my lord the king commands his servant, so will your servant do." So Mephibosheth ate at David's table, like one of the king's sons. And Mephibosheth had a young son, whose name was Mica. And all who lived in Ziba's house became Mephibosheth's servants. So Mephibosheth lived in Jerusalem, for he ate always at the king's table. Now he was lame in both his feet.

(2 Samuel 9)

20

ARE YOU GOOD ENOUGH?

(2 Samuel 9)

Are you good enough? Are you a good enough spouse, parent, employee, child, student, athlete, man, woman, or Christian? In this passage we're introduced to a man, Mephibosheth, who knew he wasn't good enough. Maybe you're convinced that you're not good enough either. Or maybe some combination of success, good looks, or self-confidence has you convinced that you are. If so, it won't always be this way. In time, you'll find yourself asking this question as well. You might try turning to the Bible to boost your self-esteem, but that won't work. The Bible actually tells us that we aren't good enough for God. It tells us that our identity, apart from God, is broken beyond our repair. We not only choose to sin, we were born sinful.[1] How is that supposed to be good news? How does God make this truth okay for Mephibosheth, for the people of God, for me, for you?

Mercy that's Good Enough for You

In the eyes of God's people, Mephibosheth was a rebel by birth. Here's what I mean. Mephibosheth was Jonathan's son which meant that he was King Saul's grandson. He was one of the last remnants of the old dynasty. In the ancient world, when a new family seized control, it was common practice to kill all the remaining males from the previous dynasty. This practice of liquidation helped solidify the new King's position and eliminate future challengers.

Was David going to purge Mephibosheth? *"And David said, 'Is there still anyone left of the house of Saul, that I may show him kindness for Jonathan's sake?'"* (9:1). Knowing that he's a "rebel," David seeks out Mephibosheth not to kill him, but to show him kindness for the sake of his friend Jonathan. Mercy means not getting the punishment we deserve. More powerful than David's mercy, God's mercy forgives even the rebellion that lives in our very DNA as sinful people.

The Bible also tells us that in addition to our rebellion, we're broken. Mephibosheth knew brokenness well, *"he [was] crippled in his feet"* (9:3). A physical disability such as this is difficult to live with at any point in history, but especially in ancient Israel. Not only did Mephibosheth lack modern medical care and aid such as a wheelchair, he was also barred, according to biblical law, from approaching God's presence. Leviticus taught that it was not safe for the crippled to come before a holy and perfect God.[2]

But what does King David do? He calls Mephibosheth to him and says, *"Do not fear"* (9:7). Why? David had experienced unconditional love from Mephibosheth's father and had promised to do the same for his family. Additionally, David has been called to display God's love in a new way that anticipates Jesus. This is why Romans tells us that while we were still enemies and sinners (like Mephibosheth) God showed love to us in Jesus.[3] It's also why Hebrews tells us that Jesus can sympathize with our weakness and that through his perfection we can safely come into a perfect God's presence.[4] We're not good enough for God's mercy, but through Jesus, God's mercy is good enough to forgive us and overcome our weakness.

In the sixteenth century, masquerade balls became the sign of high society across Europe. Royalty, lords and ladies, and the upper crust of society would gather together to eat lavish food, mingle, and dance all while wearing masks. Only at the end of the night would all the masks be taken off so that the guests could discover who it was that they had been dancing, eating, and speaking with.

While these dances are no longer popular, I'd argue that churches often act like they are. How easy is it to come to church and smile, tell everyone that you're "doing great," shake your head at sin, and then leave without taking off the mask that reveals your brokenness and rebellion? By wearing our masks we're trying to convince the world that God accepts us because we're good. This isn't true, and it's not helpful for others. So will you risk it? Will you risk admitting that you're far worse than everyone knows? Only when you risk this will you be able to celebrate that God's mercy towards you if far greater than anyone might expect. Let's take off the masks; God's mercy is enough.

Grace that's Good Enough for You

If mercy means not getting the punishment we deserve, grace means receiving goodness far beyond what we deserve. Before David found him, Mephibosheth had been living in hiding. David demands that Mephibosheth receive something better, *"Then the king called Ziba... and said... 'All that belonged to Saul... I have given to [Mephibosheth]. And you and your sons and your servants shall till the land for him and shall bring in the produce, that your master's grandson may have bread to eat'* (9:9–10). David didn't just spare Mephibosheth, he gave him the servants and vast lands of his grandfather (that rightfully belonged to David at this point) so that all of his immediate needs could be met.

But as it's always true with grace, there's more. While we all have immediate needs, the wise know that there are deeper needs within us all. While Mephibosheth now had wealth, he was still a grown man who was referred to as *lame* and *crippled,* and who called himself a *dead dog.* Worse yet, he was fatherless. Mephibosheth's greatest need was not wealth but love and family. David provides these. He calls Mephibosheth by his name, not his condition, and made sure that he *"ate at David's table, like one of the king's sons"* (9:11). Mephibosheth is invited to the place of honor and glory in the presence of the king and becomes like a son of the king. Why did David do this? Yes, he was keeping a promise to an old friend, but he was also sharing the overabundance of grace that he had received from God.

1 Samuel 9 is truly one of the most heartwarming and joy-filled moments in David's story. Why then did we focus on the pain and brokenness of Mephibosheth's life? Because this story can only bring us the healing balm of the gospel if we too have tried, failed, and surrendered to God our attempts to be good enough. When we understand this, we joyfully realize that "We are the Lord's Mephibosheths, and there is absolutely no reason why we should be eating continually at the King's table."[5] And yet by grace, we do. Our neediness doesn't save us. But, unless we admit our need, we'll never receive the mercy and grace of Jesus that finally frees us of the need to prove our worth. Let's rest in that today.

Pause for a Moment

Reflect: Where in your life are you striving to prove yourself right now?

Request: Ask God to remind you of your need for him and the sufficiency of his mercy and grace through Christ Jesus.

Respond: Find a way to give both mercy and grace to someone else today as a reflection of what Jesus has done for you.

After this the king of the Ammonites died, and Hanun his son reigned in his place. And David said, "I will deal loyally with Hanun... as his father dealt loyally with me." So David sent by his servants to console him... But the princes... said to Hanun their lord, "Do you think... David... is honoring your father? Has not David sent his servants to you to search the city and to spy it out and to overthrow it?" So Hanun took David's servants and shaved off half the beard of each and cut off their garments in the middle... and sent them away. When it was told David, he sent to meet them, for the men were greatly ashamed... When the Ammonites saw that they had become a stench to David, the Ammonites sent and hired the Syrians... And when David heard of it, he sent Joab and all the host of the mighty men... When Joab saw that the battle was set against him both in front and in the rear, he chose some of the best men of Israel and arrayed them against the Syrians. The rest... he put in the charge of Abishai... And... said, "If the Syrians are too strong for me, then you shall help me, but if the Ammonites are too strong for you, then I will... help you. Be of good courage, and let us be courageous for our people, and for the cities of our God, and may the LORD do what seems good to him."... the Syrians... fled... And... the Ammonites... likewise fled... And Hadadezer sent... the Syrians who were beyond the Euphrates... against David... the Syrians fled before Israel... And when all the kings who were servants of Hadadezer saw that they had been defeated... they made peace with Israel and became subject to them. So the Syrians were afraid to save the Ammonites anymore.
(2 Samuel 10)

21

ASSUMING THE WORST

(2 Samuel 10)

Miscommunication can be funny. A French-Canadian entrepreneur created the snowmobile but the intended company name "Ski-Dog" became "Ski-Doo" after a typo. The words evoke a slightly different mental image.[1] Nevertheless, the company has still experienced great success. Often, miscommunication causes problems. Kellog's All-Bran cereal failed miserably when it launched in Sweden. The problem? When Kellog's translated the product name into Swedish, it selected words meaning, "Burnt Farmer Cereal."[2] While this mistake led to financial loss, miscommunications during the Cold War nearly lead to nuclear strikes on multiple occasions. It's important to be understood.

Unfortunately, Christians in the West are being misunderstood more and more frequently. It's common for our neighbors to assume the worst about us. Our faith is no longer seen as respectable. Sometimes this happens because the Church fails to live consistently with the Gospel. Sometimes this happens because our neighbors do not understand the Gospel. Today, King David is misunderstood and attacked as he carries out his calling. What's a believer to do when the world assumes the worst?

Trusting God's Ways

When King David hears news of an ally's death, he intends to treat the ally's son with honor and respect: *"I will deal loyally with Hanun the son of Nahash, as his father dealt loyally with me"* (10:2). The key word here is *loyalty* which describes God's faithful love. It's the same word used to describe David's faithfulness to Mephibosheth, on account of his father Jonathan, in 2 Samuel 9. These two stories weave together a picture of David, as God's King, reflecting God's love both inside and outside the kingdom.

Indeed, God's love calls for a particular kind of treatment of others, even if it's rejected: *"But the princes. . . said to Hanun their lord, 'Do you think. . . David. . . is honoring your father? Has not David sent his servants to you to search the city and to spy it out and to overthrow it?' So Hanun took David's servants and shaved off half the beard of each and cut off their garments in the middle. . . and sent them away"* (10:3–4). The Ammonites assume the worst, reject David's loyalty, and shame his men by removing the outward sign of their masculinity (beards) and exposing their private parts. This type of behavior was tantamount to a declaration of war, which indeed came quickly.

Don't miss what just happened. David obeyed God, shared gospel love with an outsider, and watched as it all backfired on him. Doing things God's way just made David's life much more difficult. Should he have done otherwise? Absolutely not. David doesn't miss a beat as he shows compassion on his shamed men, giving them time to regain their dignity (10:5). David's continued *loyalty* reminds us that no matter the immediate outcome, God's ways are the only ways we are called to walk in.

Trusting God's Plan

Trusting God's ways requires trusting his plan. This is easy in theory, but hard in practice. David quickly finds himself in a major battle in which he's out-numbered, out-gunned (the Ammonites hire professional soldiers), and then trapped (10:9). To the reader today, this seems like just another battle. But, at this moment, David's life and God's work on earth hung in the balance.

Unexpectedly, the focus of the story turns to General Joab who does what he was made by God to do: lead the forces of Israel in battle. Joab executes a daring plan that involves splitting up his army not into equal halves but into his special forces and the general ranks. God uses this plan, combined with Joab's gripping *and* theologically astute speech, to lead Israel to victory. God, of course, is not surprised. As Joab so accurately stated, God does "*what seems good to him*" (10:12).

Like Joab, we don't always know how God's plan is going to turn out. John Calvin put it this way, "God does not give particular promises about this or that to his children. We certainly [know]... That God will never abandon us, and that in the end he will show that our hope in him was not in vain... Nevertheless, we must remain in suspense about many things."[3] In this instance, Joab couldn't have known for sure that victory was coming. But he did know that God would ultimately accomplish his plan. The same is true for us. We'd all prefer specific insight and promises about every detail of our lives, but we are instead called to trust the Father's plan while fulfilling the role he's given us to play. We don't know which battles we'll win and which we'll lose, but we do know that He will win the ultimate war.

Trusting God's Power

Although God allows his kingdom to come under siege, we must never see this as a sign of weakness. Psalm 2 captures this truth: "Why do the nations rage and the peoples plot in vain. . . against the LORD and against his Anointed. . . He who sits in the heavens laughs. . . he will speak to them in his wrath, and terrify them in his fury, saying, 'As for me, I have set my King on Zion. . . [He] shall break them with a rod of iron and dash them in pieces like a potter's vessel.' " God *laughs* at anyone and any culture that thinks it can challenge his power. Nothing will overcome his hand or the Davidic line. God's power simply will not permit it.

The Syrians attack again and learn this lesson the hard way, *"So the Syrians were afraid to save the Ammonites anymore"* (10:19). But it's not just external enemies who challenge God's power and plan. The Davidic line itself will begin to teeter and fail. David will betray the people of God with his own sin. Today the Church is mocked, slandered, and attacked. Worse yet, the Church sometimes invites this treatment when it is self-destructive and hypocritical. Even so, the power of God will prevail.

Discouraged Christians are often tempted to doubt these things. We wonder if God's ways are outdated so we compromise our lives. We question his plan and make our own instead. We grow weary of waiting on his power and push out on our own. But God never misspeaks. Though everything might seem to fall apart, God keeps his word by keeping the line of David alive. This David will fail, but his great Descendent will come. The Descendent will walk in the way, will trust the plan, and will demonstrate the power, even in apparent death and defeat. Yes, the world rages and raves against the kingdom and the King. The world often claims victory. But we must remember, the Lord *"does what seems good to him."* And that is enough.

Pause for a Moment

Reflect: Where are you most discouraged right now?

Request: Ask God to enlarge your trust of his ways, his plans, and his power.

Respond: The next time you hear a Christian proclaiming doom, smile and humbly remind the person that the Lord, *"does what seems good to him."*

In the spring... the time when kings go out to battle, David sent Joab... and all Israel. And they ravaged the Ammonites... But David remained at Jerusalem... late one afternoon, when David arose from his couch and was walking on the roof of the king's house... he saw... a woman bathing; and the woman was very beautiful. And David... inquired about the woman. And one said, "Is not this Bathsheba, the daughter of Eliam, the wife of Uriah the Hittite?" So David sent messengers and took her, and she came to him, and he lay with her... And the woman conceived, and she... told David, "I am pregnant." So David sent word to Joab, "Send me Uriah..." And Joab sent Uriah to David... Then David said... "Go down to your house and wash your feet."... But Uriah slept at the door of the king's house... Uriah said... "The ark and Israel... dwell in booths, and my lord Joab and the servants of my lord are camping in the open field. Shall I then go to my house, to eat and to drink and to lie with my wife? As you live... I will not do this thing."... In the morning David wrote a letter to Joab and sent it by the hand of Uriah. In the letter he wrote, "Set Uriah in the forefront of the hardest fighting, and then draw back from him, that he may be struck down, and die." And as Joab was besieging the city, he assigned Uriah to the place where... there were valiant men... Uriah the Hittite... died... When the wife of Uriah heard that... her husband was dead, she lamented over her husband. And when the mourning was over, David... brought her to his house, and she became his wife and bore him a son. But the thing that David had done displeased the LORD.

(2 Samuel 11)

THE FALL OF THE KING

(2 Samuel 11)

There's no way to ease into this. This *is* the darkest hour of David's life. It's the type of situation that makes you question everything you've learned about David. But make no mistake, our lives and our hearts aren't all that different. We too want more than we have. We too are rarely satisfied. Like David, and Adam and Eve before him, we've seen forbidden temptation and swallowed it whole. It may be an old problem, but it's just as real today as it was for David. We simply want more than God. And this always leads to disaster. What hope is there for us in the face of such temptation and sin?

The Good Law

What's the purpose of God's law? Many Christians believe that the law exists to punish evil and convict us of sin. This is true, but there's more. The law also has a positive side; it reveals how life works best. The law teaches us how to flourish by living according to God's design.

David knew all of this and rejoiced that the law was perfect, beautiful, and refreshing to the soul.[1] But this is where

David and every believer are tested. Do we really believe that God's law is good and that it exists for our good? At this point, David wasn't so sure. *"He saw from the roof a woman bathing; and the woman was very beautiful. And David sent and inquired about the woman. And one said, 'Is not this Bathsheba... the wife of Uriah the Hittite?'"* (11:2–3) In this moment, David needed to remember that the law, God's Word itself, was whispering warnings to him. Job was warning David to guard his eyes from lust, his Psalms were warning him that only God could satisfy, Moses warned that many wives lead kings astray, and the Ten Commandments warned him that coveting this woman, stealing a man's wife, and committing adultery were all rebellion against God.[2]

Make no mistake, David knew the law but valued his lust for Bathsheba more than his relationship with God, *"So David sent messengers and took her, and she came to him, and he lay with her"* (11:4). Like David, we often know what the law says, but we forget that it's a gift, for our good, to save us from disaster. We must not only know this good law, but also obey it.

The Guiding Call

While the law tells us *what* to do, our calling tells us *who* we are. Everyone has a calling. Genesis tells us that we were all created by God to serve him. Through his work on the cross, Jesus makes that possible by forgiving our sins and transforming all who believe into beloved children of God. Additionally, we have more particular callings from God as men or women, as parents and children, and often as employees and employers. Like ours, David's chief calling was to live life as a loved and redeemed child of God. Specifically, he was called to lead the people of God as their godly king.

Callings help direct our priorities. Sadly, the text suggests that David was forgetting this too, *"In the spring. . . the time when kings go out to battle, David sent Joab. . . and all Israel. . . But David remained at Jerusalem. . . late one afternoon. . . David arose from his couch. . ."* (11:1–2). While there's nothing wrong with rest, David isn't doing his job. Instead of leading his people into battle, he's drooling on the couch. David's misplaced priorities quickly turn into an affair and a surprise pregnancy.

What could David do now? Wrongly, David tries to use two wrongs to make a right. He calls Bathsheba's husband home from the war and tells him to go home for the night. David tries to give this innocent man a "date night" so that no one will question the timing of the pregnancy.

At this point it's helpful to remember who David's trying to trick. David actually knew Uriah personally! Uriah was a member of David's special forces and David likely led Uriah, a foreigner, to faith in the Lord several years before this![3] The depth of David's sin in this movement can hardly be overstated. It's a betrayal of the highest order! Unlike David, Uriah knows his calling, *"The ark and Israel and Judah dwell in booths. . . Shall I then go to my house, to eat and to drink and to lie with my wife? As you live, and as your soul lives, I will not do this thing"* (11:11). In this dark hour, the King of Israel's faith fails while the faith of a Hittite shines bright.

The Only Hope

What happens though, when we do get it all wrong? From the beginning, God has declared hope for sinners. From the very first sin in Eden, God promised to save his children.[4] David would remember this and say: "Blessed is the one whose transgressions are forgiven, whose sins are covered."[5] Once again he would confess, "you forgave the [guilt] of my sin." There is hope for sinners in God alone.

But David hasn't remembered this yet. In fact, David is in a bind. He's broken the law, committed adultery, impregnated Bathsheba, and now Uriah won't play along with the cover-up. Instead of hoping in God, David trusts in more sin. *"David wrote a letter to Joab... 'Set Uriah in the forefront of the hardest fighting, and then draw back from him, that he may be struck down and die'"* (11:14–15). If Uriah wouldn't go along with David's plan, he'd just have to be killed. Joab, a shady schemer himself, plays along and godly Uriah dies. David, thinking he's gotten away with it all, takes Bathsheba, marries her, and she gives birth to a son. But there is no hope for sin apart from God. *"The thing that David had done displeased the LORD"* (11:27).

These days of David are dark. There will be serious consequences. There always are. Thankfully though, David's ultimate standing with God was never about his goodness and God's people will find a greater king, who, instead of sinning, will cover the sins of his people with his perfect blood. This David will say, "I give my sheep eternal life. No one will snatch them out of my hand."[6] Yes, David will face consequences the rest of his life for this sin and we too must deal with the results of our disobedience. But even in the darkness, the children of God can know that our King never lets go. If we are his, he will pull us back, draw us to repentance, and restore us. He will not let David go.

Pause for a Moment

Reflect: Are you surprised by David's actions? Are you ever surprised by your own sin?

Request: Ask God to show you where you need to repent of sin today.

Respond: Spend some time today evaluating your relationship with God. Consider your beliefs and behavior. Take heart, if you trust in Jesus to save you, even with an ounce of faith, you can rest in his promises of forgiven sin and a transformed life.

And the LORD sent Nathan to David. He. . . said. . . "There were two men. . . one rich and the other poor. . . the poor man had nothing but one little. . . lamb. . . and it grew up with him and with his children. It used to. . . lie in his arms, and it was like a daughter to him. Now there came a traveler to the rich man, and he was unwilling to take one of his own flock. . . to prepare for the guest. . . but he took the poor man's lamb and prepared it. . ." Then David's anger was greatly kindled. . . and he said. . .

"As the LORD lives, the man who has done this deserves to die. . ." Nathan said to David, "You are the man! Thus says the LORD. . . 'I anointed you king. . . and I delivered you out of the hand of Saul. And I gave you. . . the house of Israel and of Judah. . . Why have you despised the word of the LORD, to do what is evil in his sight? You have struck down Uriah. . . and have taken his wife. . . Now therefore the sword shall never depart from your house. . . And I will take your wives before your eyes and give them to your neighbor. . ." David said. . . "I have sinned against the LORD." And Nathan said. . . "The LORD. . . has put away your sin; you shall not die. Nevertheless. . . the child who is born to you shall die. . ." David therefore sought God on behalf of the child. And. . . fasted. . . On the seventh day the child died. . . Then David. . . washed and anointed himself. . . and. . . went into the house of the LORD and worshiped. . . He said, "While the child was. . . alive, I fasted and wept. . . But now he is dead. . . Can I bring him back again? I shall go to him, but he will not return to me." Then David comforted his wife, Bathsheba. . . and she bore a son. . . Solomon. And the LORD loved him and sent a message by Nathan. . . So he called his name Jedidiah, because of the LORD.
(2 Samuel 12:1–25)

23

THE RESTORATION OF THE KING

(2 Samuel 12)

A fast-food coma. A late-night Netflix binge. A caffeine short-age. Driver fatigue. A sugar crash. New parent exhaustion. Finals cramming. What do all these situations have in common? They cause drowsiness. However, even if we listed fifty more sleep-inducing scenarios we might miss the biggest one: sin. While some types of sin literally cause drowsiness, all sin creates spiritual dullness and fatigue. In fact, sin, or dis-obedience to God, can have a powerful numbing effect on our senses. The more you sin the easier it gets. Spiritually, some Christians spend months, even years, doing the spiritual equivalent of sleepwalking.

After committing adultery and murder, David found him-self in a spiritual slumber that lasted over nine months. During this entire time, David was unwilling to repent. But then God spoke and everything changed. Indeed, Jesus prom-ises that when he calls out to us we, who believe, will recognize his voice. And that's because God loves awaking his sleeping saints and restoring them to the paths of life. So how does God get our attention when we're drowsy with sin?

Waking Up through Conviction

Due to the severity of David's condition, God initiates a wake-up call through the prophet Nathan. Using subtle tactics meant to stir David's heart, Nathan asks David to decide a "legal case" between a rich man and a poor man. David is quickly drawn into the story. The poor man has little, just a small lamb that he loves like a child. The rich man, too greedy to enjoy his own abundance, steals the poor man's lamb and kills it to feed his guests. For the first time in many months, David's sense of justice is kindled as he declares a judgment against the rich man. David thinks the story is about another man, but God is at work, preparing him for conviction. *"Nathan said to David, 'You are the man'"* (12:7). How quickly the judge becomes the judged!

This is how the gospel works. It only becomes real when it ceases to be purely academic. Real conviction leads to real confession. *"David said to Nathan, 'I have sinned against the LORD'"* (12:13). No excuses, no justifying, no downplaying, David knows that above all else, he has betrayed the Lord. Only through conviction can God's healing work begin.

Waking Up through Consequences

God also lets us face the consequences of our sin so that we can understand it's severity. There's nothing casual about disobeying God. Whether we see it or not, sin sends ripples of destruction all around us. As a good father, God wants David to see these so that he can grow. He tells David that because he embraced violence, his family will see violence. Because David destroyed a family, his family will be disrupted. Because he stole a wife, his wives will be stolen. And because David did all of this publicly, without hesitation, all these consequences will be public (12:12). David is learning that sin is never private, personal, or minor.

Often, Christians assume that forgiveness cancels out consequences. But that's not how God works. David receives both, *"The LORD has put away your sin; you shall not die. Nevertheless. . . the child who is born to you shall die"* (12:13–14). Our consequences do not condemn us, rather they remind us that there is a cost to forgiveness. This cost, as we see throughout the Bible, always must be born by another, and in this case, a son of David must die.[1]

This is part of the problem with sin, it makes wonderful promises without telling us the cost. A dad feels the pull and desire of clicking on that pop-up ad, but sin fails to mention that his actions will introduce his son to a lifetime of pornography addiction. A mother feels the embarrassment of her daughter's sloppiness, but sin fails to mention that her constant image-focused comments will inspire an eating disorder. A young employee tastes the thrill of success, but sin doesn't mention that a life lived for work will leave them empty, alone, and a slave to performance. Don't ignore the consequences of your sin; let them guide you to repentance!

Waking Up through Compassion

As David faces the sickening consequence of watching his son die he turns to prayer. *"David therefore sought God on behalf of the child"* (12:16). By grace, David does what any Christian parent should do, but his son *still* dies. Surprisingly, once the bad news arrives David gets up, cleans himself up, and then worships. How is he able to do this?

David explains, *"While the child was still alive, I fasted and wept, for I said, 'Who knows whether the* LORD *will be gracious to me, that the child may live? But now he is dead. Why should I fast? Can I bring him back again? I shall go to him, but he will not return to me'"* (12:22–23). David sought God's grace and even though God said no to this specific request, David knew he would find comfort in God's presence.

In time, David sees God's compassion in unmistakable ways. For one, God, in his infinite grace, allows David and Bathsheba to have another child, Solomon. We're told that, *"The* LORD *loved him... So he [also] called his name Jedidiah"* (12:24–25). David names his son "beloved of the LORD." Second, God gives David a chance to return as the leader of Israel's armies and secure a major victory later in this chapter (12:26–31). Even in and after our sin, God's compassion and love are at work to awaken us to his goodness.

If God is so compassionate we ask, why does he make such a big deal about sin and repentance? It's safe to say that God's goal is not venting his anger, making our lives difficult, or punishing us. No, his goal is restoration from the evil and darkness that sin covers us with. Restoration simply can't happen without the grace of conviction, consequences, and his ongoing compassion. God won't settle for just forgiving us, he wants to fully restore us. And he can do this because the price for our sin has been paid by another. Another son of David had to die. But this time the son of David was also the Son of God. Jesus was killed and struck down by the Father, in our place, and rose from the dead so that we might be right with God, despite our sin. This gift is available to all. Sin is a bad business, but repentance is a good one.

Pause for a Moment

Reflect: The great Reformer Martin Luther said that all of the Christian life is one of repentance.[2] What do you think he meant by that?

Request: Ask God to give you the gift of repentance. Ask him to show you your sin and how to turn from it towards him.

Respond: If you are a parent of younger children make sure your discipline always has the goal of restoration and not simply punishment. If you still live at home, thank your parents for their discipline even if it's imperfect.

Now Absalom, David's son, had a beautiful sister, whose name was Tamar... Amnon, David's son, loved her. And... was so tormented that he made himself ill because... she was a virgin, and it seemed impossible to... do anything to her... Jonadab... said to him, "Lie down on your bed and pretend to be ill... say...'Let my sister come.' " ... Tamar went to her brother Amnon's house... he took hold of her and said to her, "Come, lie with me, my sister." She answered... "No, my brother, do not violate me, for such a thing is not done in Israel..." But he would not listen to her, and... he violated her... Then Amnon hated her... so that the hatred with which he hated her was greater than the love with which he had loved her. And Amnon said to her, "Get up! Go!" But she said to him, "No... for this wrong in sending me away is greater..." But he would not listen to her. He called... and said, "Put this woman out of my presence..." And Tamar put ashes on her head... And her brother Absalom said to her, "Has Amnon your brother been with you? Now hold your peace, my sister..." So Tamar lived, a desolate woman, in her brother Absalom's house. When King David heard of all these things, he was very angry... After two full years Absalom had sheepshearers at Baal-hazor... and Absalom invited all the king's sons... Then Absalom commanded his servants, "when I say to you, 'Strike Amnon,' then kill him. Do not fear; have I not commanded you... " So the servants of Absalom did to Amnon as Absalom had commanded. Then all the king's sons... fled... And the king also and all his servants wept very bitterly... So Absalom fled and went to Geshur, and was there three years. And the spirit of the king longed to go out to Absalom...
(2 Samuel 13:1–39)

24

WHEN DARKNESS REIGNS

(2 Samuel 13)

A young Ohio couple decided to rob a bank. Hiding their faces, they gave the teller a note, took a few big wads of cash, and fled. It worked. Nearly a month passed. The police had no leads. The couple was so excited that they posted pictures of the cash on Facebook. Can you guess what happened next? The police showed up, took the money, and threw the couple into jail on felony charges.[1] What were they thinking? How could they forget that robbing a bank is a serious offense?

It's easy to poke fun at this couple. It really is. However, we buy into the same line of thinking daily. We too forget how destructive sin is. We forget that sin affects our lives, our hearts, our relationships, and our communities. We demonstrate our forgetfulness in the shows we watch, the either obsessive or neglectful care we give our bodies, the words we choose, the thoughts we entertain, and the way we spend our time and money. In this last chapter we watched as sin put David into a spiritual slumber. In this chapter we turn to the consequences of this as they play out in real life. As we do so, we'll be seeking to learn how to push back against sin and pursue God while waiting for him to destroy sin once and for all.

Fleeing Sin's Call

Amnon was David's oldest son and heir to the throne. Like his father, Amnon was drawn towards something that he couldn't have. In this case, it was his beautiful half-sister Tamar. Sin's pull was strong. *"Amnon was so tormented that he made himself ill... for... it seemed impossible to... do anything to her"* (13:2). The temptation was so dark that Amnon wasn't even interested in a relationship, just doing something *to her.* We know what that something was.

Sin can do more than urge, it can also persuade. Although Amnon couldn't figure out how to act, his cousin, a *crafty man*, gave him an easy way to pursue it. *"Lie down on your bed and pretend to be ill. And when your father comes to see you, say to him, 'Let my sister Tamar come and give me bread to eat' "* (13:5). How easily we're persuaded to do what we already want to do. Ammon, like his father before him, listens to sin's call. He, however, takes his sister by force. She tries to reason with him. He rapes her.

We may not see ourselves in Amnon, but we too play around with sin, entertaining its promises until it's too late. This is a problem. As pastor John Owen wisely counseled, "Be killing sin or it will be killing you."[2] We must actively avoid sin. We must say no to its offers. We must turn to God's Word. We must hold on to God's surer promises. We must move on to something better.[3] We can't play around.

Fleeing Sin's Condemnation

But what happens after you've sinned? Sin tends to change tactics by moving from encouragement ("Do it!") to condemnation ("There's no hope!"). Amnon experienced this after raping his sister. *"Then Amnon hated her with very great hatred, so that the hatred with which he hated her was greater than the love with which he had loved her. And Amnon said to her, 'Get up! Go!'"* (13:15). Amnon's lust turned to hate as he throws her out.

Because of the way shame functioned in the ancient world, a raped woman like Tamar tragically had almost no chance at marriage or a normal life anymore. In fact, as awful as it sounds to us, her best hope, in this cultural situation, was having her brother marry her. Instead of moving in this direction, Amnon kicks her to the curb and locks the door behind her. Sin leads to more sin. Indeed, sin maliciously tells both the offender and the victim that they are worthless.

Sin not only condemns our hope, it also paralyzes our obedience. What will David do when he hears about this? Will he bring justice? *"When King David heard of all these things, he was very angry"* (13: 21). That's a good start, but we get nothing more. David the giant killer sits back passively. Why? Because he's watching his son repeat his own sin and lacks the courage to speak truth into an area he failed in. What Nathan said comes true; David's sin is wrecking his family. It tells Amnon that he can't make things right. It tells Tamar that her life is over. It tells David that he's a hypocrite who can't lead. But we know that the Gospel offers forgiveness for sinners, cleansing for those sinned against, and hope for hypocrites. Knowing God means we don't have to listen to sin's condemnation.

Fleeing Sin's Comfort

Sin seeks to complete its trifecta of disaster by promising us that the only comfort found in condemnation is more sin. As Amnon slinks away in his guilt, Tamar is consoled by her other brother Absalom. He hates what Amnon has done and is convinced by sin that revenge is the only comfort to be found. With calm and cold-hearted calculation, Absalom waits two years before coming up with a plan to butcher Amnon at a party. The plan works perfectly, and Amnon is slayed. But the comfort of sin is always temporary. Absalom is forced to flee. David himself finds temporary comfort in not dealing with Absalom and simply issuing a lifetime banishment. This inaction will cost David two sons.

Sin calls, it condemns those who listen, and then it offers comfort by repeating the process. But the comfort never lasts. Even though we know this, we fall for it, sometimes often. This is why we need the One who always flees sin's call, trusting instead in God's Word, who always flees sin's condemnation, living perfectly instead, and who always flees false comfort, obeying God to the point of death instead. Because of this Jesus, you can say no to sin as well, because his Word dwells within you. Because of this Jesus, you also can flee condemnation, because he took it for you on the cross. And because of this Jesus, you can replace the comfort of sin with the comfort of being received as a child of God.

Pause for a Moment

Reflect: Which part of sin's trifecta (call, condemnation, or comfort) tends to ensnare you the most?

Request: Ask Jesus to fight temptation with and for you. He is a mighty warrior who defends his children fiercely. Trust his power for the battle.

Respond: Notice when temptation comes today. Try to avoid it. When you see it say "no." Remember God's word and his better promises. Turn to something better.

After this Absalom got... a chariot... and fifty men to run before him. And Absalom used to... stand beside... she gate. And when any man had a dispute... Absalom would... say, "... See, your claims are good... but there is no man designated by the king to hear you... Oh that I were judge in the land!"... So

Absalom stole the hearts of the men of Israel... And the conspiracy grew strong... And a messenger came to David, saying, "The hearts... of Israel have gone after Absalom." Then David said to... his servants... "let us flee, or else there will be no escape..."... Then the king said to Ittai the Gittite, "you are a foreigner... shall I today make you wander about with us... Go back... and may the LORD show steadfast love and faithfulness to you." But Ittai answered... "As the LORD lives, and as my lord the king lives, wherever my lord the king shall be, whether for death or for life, there also will your servant be"... And Abiathar... and... Zadok came... bearing the ark... Then the king said... "Carry the ark of God back into the city. If I find favor in the eyes of the LORD, he will bring me back... But if he says, 'I have no pleasure in you,' behold, here I am, let him do to me what seems good to him... See, I will wait at the fords... until word comes from you to inform me." So Zadok and Abiathar carried the ark... back... But David went up... the Mount of Olives, weeping... barefoot and with his head covered. And all the people... covered their heads, and they went up, weeping... And it was told David, "Ahithophel is among the conspirators..."... David said, "O LORD, please turn the counsel of Ahithophel into foolishness." Hushai... came to meet him... David said... "if you return... and say to Absalom, 'I will be your servant...' then you will defeat for me the counsel of Ahithophel."

(2 Samuel 15:1–34)

WEEPING WITH HOPE

(2 Samuel 15)

The great John Wayne, known for saying, "I'm the stuff men are made of,"[1] embodied the idea that real men don't cry. The manly Ron Swanson of the sit-com *Parks & Recreation* said this about crying: "I've only cried twice in my life and once was when I was seven and got hit by the school bus."[2] It appears that outward displays of grief, particularly from men, are rare and discouraged by our culture. Unfortunately, these sentiments are completely wrong. Christians live in a broken world, and because of this we must acknowledge that there is a time to grieve and weep. Choosing to deny or ignore these feelings is a denial of reality. And it's not just a problem for men. Most Christians grapple with the pressure of trying to keep it all together.

In 2 Samuel 15, David and the people of God can do nothing but weep. And that's OK. The Bible calls us to weep over sin and tragedy, but it also calls us to do so with hope. In his first letter to the Thessalonians, the Apostle Paul comforts a church that's grieving. He gives them permission to mourn but also instructs them to grieve differently than the world, because of the hope that they have in Jesus. How will God help David and his people do this? How will he help us?

Not Alone

Grief tends to isolate us and make us feel alone. David felt this. His banished son Absalom wormed his way back home in 2 Samuel 14. Then, using careful calculations, he convinced the people that he looked and acted more like a king than David. *"So Absalom stole the hearts of the men of Israel"* (15:6). In short time, Absalom seized the throne. Feeling rejected, David was forced to flee.

In his grace, God reminded David that he wasn't alone. In fact, as David's supporters left the city with him, he noticed one particular foreigner, Ittai the Gittite. David asks Ittai why he's sticking with him. David graciously and sincerely gives him permission to turn back. Ittai's answer shocks David. *"As the LORD lives, and as my lord the king lives, wherever my lord the king lives, wherever my lord the king shall be, whether for death or for life, there also will your servant be"* (15:21). This is a Philistine man from the hometown of Goliath, he owes nothing to David, and he has little children with him (15:22). Even so, he swears a covenant oath of loyalty to David and it becomes clear that he's a believer, a man loyal to both David and David's God. Through the loyalty and faith of this Philistine convert, God is reminding David that he has not forsaken him. David is not alone.

In the midst of suffering, we love to ask "Why?" We would do well to ask instead, "Who is with me?" For every Christian can confidently answer, "Christ." And, in most situations, we can also add "The body of Christ." You are not alone. You can weep with hope.

Not in Charge

Because we often feel alone in grief, we're tempted to think that we need to take charge. Surely David felt the need to stop Absalom. David was supposed to be King, how could it be that he was now exiled? As he considers these things, the priests arrived with what could be David's last chance to seize control: the ark. David's grief must have made the prospect of wielding this weapon against Absalom enticing. But God's grace guides David as he speaks to the priests, "*Carry the ark of God back into the city. If I find favor in the eyes or the LORD, he will bring me back and let me see both it and his dwelling place. But if he says, 'I have no pleasure in you.' Behold, here I am, let him do to me what seems good to him'* " (15:25–26). What a beautiful thing it is when God's servants resign themselves to God's will. David sends the ark back knowing that God cannot be used like a superstitious weapon, rather, he must be trusted.

Like David, we might want or even crave control. But if we had it, everything would rest upon our wisdom and power. Good thing it doesn't. We can weep with hope trusting in God's plan.

Not Hopeless

Sometimes the floor falls out from beneath us. In a genuine expression of utter grief, David climbs up the Mount of Olives, weeping, barefoot, with head covered. This is when the bomb drops. David's top advisor, Ahithophel, a brilliant man who understands David's tactics better than anyone else, has become a traitor. David responds in the only (and best) way that he can, he prays: *"O LORD, please turn the counsel of*

Ahithophel into foolishness" (15:31). Hope is not lost. God hears his children. Out of nowhere, another of David's advisors, Hushai, shows up. He is no traitor. And David sees the answered prayer. Hushai is sent back as a double agent to work for Absalom, to counter the advice of Ahithophel, and to relay information back to David. The situation is still bad, but God gives his servant hope, one glimmer at a time.

During the bombing of England in World War Two, thousands of children were orphaned. Even after they were rescued, the children struggled because they had suffered so much. Many of them couldn't sleep, afraid that again they would wake up without shelter and food. Finally, someone had a great idea. Each child was given a slice of bread to hold each night. With the bread grasped tightly in their tiny hands, the children slept through the night. The bread was a reminder that today they had eaten and tomorrow they would eat again.[3]

Due to our sin and the brokenness of this world, many of us struggle with anxiety, grief, fear, and despair. Thankfully, another David climbed that same Mount of Olives two thousand years ago, groaning over his coming suffering as a close friend betrayed him to the enemy. This time, however, God's plan allowed for the second David, Jesus, to die. But because he rose from the dead, you and I are able to come to the communion table and receive a little piece of bread as a sign and seal that today there is hope and tomorrow there will be as well because we have Christ. Yes, Christians weep. But we weep with hope. We have Christ, and more importantly, Christ has us.

Pause for a Moment

Reflect: Do you let yourself grieve? Do you share your grief with others?

Request: Pray for those you know to be grieving. Ask for Jesus to comfort them with his presence.

Respond: Identify one of the people you prayed for and find a small way to share the kindness of Jesus with them.

Then David. . . sent out the army. . . And the king ordered Joab and Abishai and Ittai, "Deal gently for my sake with the young man Absalom". . .And the men of Israel were defeated. . . by the servants of David. . . the battle spread over the face of all the country, and the forest devoured more people that day than the sword. . . Absalom was riding on his mule, and the mule went under the thick branches of a great oak, and his head caught fast in the oak, and he was suspended between heaven and earth. Joab. . . took three javelins in his hand and thrust them into the heart of Absalom. . . And all Israel fled every one to his own home. . . Now David was sitting between the two gates. . . and the Cushite said, "Good news for my lord the king! For the LORD has delivered you this day from the hand of all who rose up against you." The king said. . . "Is it well with the young man Absalom?" And the Cushite answered, "May the enemies of my lord the king. . . be like that young man." And the king was deeply moved and went up to the chamber over the gate and wept. And as he went, he said, "O my son Absalom, my son, my son Absalom! Would I had died instead of you. . ." So the victory that day was turned into mourning for all the people. . . Then Joab came. . . to the king and said, "You have today covered with shame the faces of all your servants, who have this day saved your life. . . for today I know that if Absalom were alive and all of us were dead. . . you would be pleased. Now therefore arise, go out and speak kindly to your servants. . ." Then the king arose and took his seat in the gate. . . And all the people came before the king.
(2 Samuel 18–19:8)

26

GOD WANTS EVERYTHING

(2 Samuel 18–19:8)

Can you honestly say that you're willing to go "all in" with God? Today, David wrestles with this. He discovers that he's not comfortable handing everything over to God. Are you? The risk seems great. And yet, hard as it may be, this is exactly what the Bible calls us to do. Psalm 37 tells us to "commit everything you to do to the LORD,"[1] and Proverbs 3 calls us to "Trust in the LORD with all your heart." How can we really trust God like this? Let's be blunt. Why is God worthy of this kind of trust?

Deliverance from Enemies

Real enemies can kill you, wreck your life, and wound your soul. This is why we must remember that God always defeats the enemies of his people. Here's David's situation: He's on the run from his son Absalom, and he's gathered his men for one last battle. David knew that God had always kept his promises regarding enemies in the past. The same holds true today: *"And the men of Israel were defeated there by the servants of David. . . and the forest devoured more people that day than the sword"* (18:7–8). Even creation joins in as God defeats David's enemies.

But there's a catch. God will defeat his enemies, but he will do it as he pleases. This means that he will do it on his schedule and according to his ways. David wanted God's help but he had stipulations, *"And [he] ordered Joab. . . 'Deal gently for my sake with the young man Absalom'"* (18:5). David wants to win, but he wants to win his way. And this involves asking his men to do the unthinkable, risking their own lives to protect the enemy in battle. As David learns, God's ways are different, "For as the heavens are higher than the earth, so are my ways higher than your ways and my thoughts than your thoughts."² God will defeat his enemies, but he will do it his way.

For Christians around the world today this is a guarantee that God will get the last word over terrorists, tyrants, hostile cultures, and hateful individuals who seek to silence God and those who follow him. But it doesn't mean that we will see that moment in this life or that it will go according to our preferences. Nevertheless, God will deliver us from our enemies. We can fully trust that.

Deliverance from Idols

As dangerous as Absalom's army was, Absalom himself posed the greater danger to David. Why? He'd become an idol. An idol is something we love, trust, and serve before God. We've seen evidence of David's idolatry recently. David more or less excused Absalom's murder of his brother, allowed his exile to end without justice or repentance, watched him start an uprising, and now wants to make sure that he doesn't die while he's trying to kill David. Is this because David knows he's partially responsible for this mess? Probably. David likely had a false hope that idolizing Absalom would let him fix everything.

False hopes must be removed: *"Absalom was riding on his mule, and the mule went under the thick branches of a great oak, and his head caught fast in the oak, and he was suspended between heaven and earth..."* (18:9). In the end, Absalom's wavy locks and puffed up head got stuck in a tree. David's general Joab hears the news and gladly disobeys David, killing Absalom to end the battle and rebellion. Absalom's life ends pitifully. The false hope, the false idol, is gone. Will David see this?

In the classic American novel *Death Comes For the Archbishop*, the story is told of a brave French priest who travels across the wild American Southwest to share his faith. One particular challenge he faces is convincing a beautiful young widow to admit her age. If she doesn't publicly do so, she will forfeit her inheritance and be left destitute. Sadly, she idolized her looks: "I never could hold up my head again [if I admitted my age]. Let [them] have the money. I don't want it..." As the severity of the situation settled in she tried to compromise, "Father, what's the youngest I could possibly be [to receive the will]?"[3] Idols are hard to give up, and yet, God can be fully trusted to remove them from our lives. Which ones are you holding onto?

Deliverance from Self

Everyone wants to be delivered from their enemies. Christians claim to desire deliverance from idols. Almost no one admits that they need to be rescued from themselves. But that's exactly what David needs.

The news about Absalom's death hits David like a boulder to the stomach. *"The king was deeply moved and went up to the chamber over the gate and wept. And as he went, he said, 'O my son Absalom, my son, my son Absalom! Would I have died instead of you...'* " (18:33). On the one hand, we need to recognize a father's legitimate grief and guilt. At the same time, something unhealthy is happening here. *"So the victory that day turned into mourning for all the people... And the people stole into the city that day as people steal in who are ashamed when they flee in battle"* (19:2–3). Instead of thanking the men who risked their lives to flee and fight with him, David shames them with his idolatrous grief.

Thankfully, the coarse Joab is able to peel David's eyes off himself. *"You have today covered with shame the faces of all your servants, who have this day saved your life... I know that if Absalom were alive and all of us were dead today, then you would be pleased. Now therefore arise, go out and speak kindly to your servants..."* (19:5–7). Ending this speech with threats, Joab reminds David that the world does not revolve around him. By grace, David sees his self-destruction, stands up in repentance, and goes to his people.

In this passage, God forced David to go all in and he couldn't. David suffered and wept over his own grief and guilt. So God had to do it for him. David is a king like us, but he's not the king we need. Years later God would call a second chosen king to suffer. But this king would carry our guilt and grief saying all the while "not my will but yours."[4] Jesus is the king we need. Like David, you can't go all in, but Jesus has done it for you, bringing deliverance from enemies, idols, and self. And so, as you hear God's call to go all in, you've got nothing to lose or fear because you've already gained everything in Christ.

Pause for a Moment

Reflect: How often do you ask God to save you from enemies? Idols? Self?

Request: Ask God to reveal your deepest idols. He promises to do so.

Respond: Go all in today. Identify a real struggle in your life and make a tangible effort to pursue growth, health, and repentance.

David. . . fought against the Philistines. And David grew weary. And Ishbi-benob, one of the descendants of the giants. . . thought to kill David. But Abishai. . . came to his aid and attacked the Philistine and killed him. Then David's men swore to him, "You shall no longer go out with us to battle, lest you quench the lamp of Israel". . . These are the names of the mighty men whom David had: Josheb-basshebeth. . . he was chief of the three. He wielded his spear against eight hundred whom he killed at one time. And next to him. . . was Eleazar. . . And next to him was Shammah. . . The Philistines gathered together at Lehi, where there was a plot of ground full of lentils, and the men fled from the Philistines. But he took his stand in the midst of the plot and defended it and struck down the Philistines, and the LORD worked a great victory. . . Asahel the brother of Joab was one of the thirty; Elhanan the son of Dodo of Bethlehem, Shammah of Harod, Elika of Harod, Helez the Paltite, Ira the son of Ikkesh of Tekoa, Abiezer of Anathoth, Mebunnai the Hushathite, Zalmon the Ahohite, Maharai of Netophah, Heleb the son of Baanah of Netophah, Ittai the son of Ribai of Gibeah of the people of Benjamin, Benaiah of Pirathon, Hiddai of the brooks of Gaash, Abi-albon the Arbathite, Azmaveth of Bahurim, Eliahba the Shaalbonite, the sons of Jashen, Jonathan, Shammah the Hararite, Ahiam the son of Sharar the Hararite, Eliphelet the son of Ahasbai of Maacah, Eliam the son of Ahithophel the Gilonite, Hezro of Carmel, Paarai the Arbite, Igal the son of Nathan of Zobah, Bani the Gadite, Zelek the Ammonite, Naharai of Beeroth, the armor-bearer of Joab the son of Zeruiah, Ira the Ithrite, Gareb the Ithrite, Uriah the Hittite: thirty-seven in all.

(2 Samuel 21:15–23:39)

27

DON'T FIGHT ALONE

(2 Samuel 21:15–22 & 23:8–39)

It had been a long journey and the end was in sight. But the desert heat scorched his skin, the volcanic ash burned his eyes, and the mountainous climb cramped his legs. As he paused, the fate of the world stood on the point of a knife. If Frodo did not press on and destroy the ring, evil would reign. At that moment his companion, Sam, spoke up, "Do you remember home, Mr. Frodo? It'd be spring soon, and the orchards will be in blossom, and the birds will be nestling in the hazel thicket, and they'll be sowing the summer barley in the lower fields, and eating the first of the strawberries with cream. Do you remember the taste of strawberries?"[1] Those who have watched the *Lord of the Rings* trilogy know that these simple words of remembrance from a friend, along with an outstretched hand, were exactly what Frodo needed to press on.

The fate of the world may not be upon our shoulders, but we too need help pressing on. Sometimes we need help when life, like a long and slow snowstorm, keeps pilling worry, pain, and disappointment upon us until we feel crushed. At other times the need comes when we are suddenly faced with a tragedy so shocking, so wrong, or so inconceivable that we are left paralyzed by fear. It's in moments like these that Christians need to be reminded of God's goodness, especially in the past. Indeed, 2 Samuel gives us a beautiful record of God providing for the warriors who served David. As we look at this record, and examine those who have gone before us, what encouragement will we find so that we too can press on?

Pressing on Together

At this point in time we are well aware of David's moral and spiritual shortcomings. However, for the very first time, we are now going to see David struggle physically: "*David...fought against the Philistines. And David grew weary. And Ishbi-Benob, one of the descendants of the giants... thought to kill David*" (21:15–16). Of course, David was older now and his armor was heavy, but his weakness surprises us. He's God's Covenant King, the hero who slayed Goliath! Is some lesser giant really going to dispatch him?

At the last moment, Abishai, one of David's mighty men, jumps in and slays the giant. Without this passage, it is "possible to imagine a heroic David who does not struggle, for whom [God's] presence meant inevitable and easy victory."[2] David was safe, but only by the strength of the men God had given him. This close call prompts the army to force David into battlefield retirement. The mighty men need David to lead, and David now needs them to do the fighting.

This pattern of mutual dependency is a beautiful picture of the Church at work. Though our society looks down upon those who need help, God looks down upon the desire to live out our faith as a lone ranger. We need each other to press on. God has ordained that it be so!

Pressing on against All Odds

While we are called to lean upon one another, there are specific times when God calls us to take a stand, perhaps alone, because others have faltered.[3] This is a reoccurring theme with David's special forces. God gives them courage while others fall to fear. *"The Philistines gathered together at Lehi, where there was a plot of ground full of lentils, and the men fled from the Philistines. But [Shammah] took his stand in the midst of the plot and defended it and struck down the Philistines, and the LORD worked a great victory"* (23:11–12). When everyone else gave up, Shammah stood with courage.

How could Shammah do it? The end of the verse tells us that *"the LORD worked a great victory."* God provides supernatural courage against all odds. But he also provides the needed strength: *"[Josheb] wielded his spear against eight hundred whom he killed at one time"* (23:8). With courage, God also gave Josheb the strength to kill 800 enemies at once. There are many who read these accounts and dismiss them as legend. How could these deeds be possible? Only by God's grace. Only God could give this kind of strength. To deny these accounts is to deny the power of God.

But what about today? Does God still give strength and courage like this? He does. But we also need to remember that God wisely gives it in a way that fits the need. If you aren't spending your days rescuing the weak and defenseless on battlefields, don't expect the gift of supernatural swordsmanship. Pray for something more fitting. I'm reminded of how I've seen the gift of supernatural integrity in the life of my father who works as an attorney or the gift of supernatural service in the life of my mother who lives with excruciating chronic pain. God's gifts against all odds don't make life easy or perfect, but they do make an eternal difference. Integrity doesn't make life easy and chronic pain still is chronic pain. David's men grew weary at times, surely their hearts raced with fear, and dreams of gore likely haunted their sleep at times. Nevertheless, God calls us to push on against all odds by becoming fully dependent upon him, knowing that he gives what is needed.

Pressing On With Humility

God's gifts remind us just how desperately we need him. This chapter ends with a long list of David's thirty mighty men. While some of these men were no longer living at this point in the story, their loyalty and service had been a wonderful yet humbling gift from God to David. However, we need to remember where these men came from. Hearing of their good deeds makes it easy to forget that most of these men came to David as outlaws who were both poor and despised. They had received God's humbling grace and mercy.

David is no stranger to grace. Notice the last name in the list of mighty men: Uriah the Hittite. The man David killed to steal his wife. This is a reminder of where David has been and how he has been forgiven. God's forgiveness also helps us press on with humility. Not alone but with the body of Christ. Not just when it seems possible, but especially when you know God will have to do the heavy lifting. And finally, not in pride, but with the humility of knowing what he has provided, namely grace and forgiveness. These men imperfectly point us to the perfect One who sees to it that you finish your race. Don't forget this when the path grows difficult!

Pause for a Moment

Reflect: What role does the local church play in your life?

Request: Ask God for strength to do the things you can't. He's far more pleased with desperate reliance than proud independence.

Respond: Encourage a brother or sister in Christ today.

And David spoke to the LORD the words of this song on the day when the LORD delivered him from the hand of all his enemies... "The LORD is my rock and my fortress and my deliverer, my God... my savior; you save me from violence... For the waves of death encompassed me... the cords of Sheol entangled me; the snares of death confronted me. In my distress I called upon the LORD... From his temple he heard my voice... Then the earth reeled and rocked... because he was angry. Smoke went up from his nostrils... He bowed the heavens and came down... Out of the brightness before him coals of fire flamed forth. The LORD thundered from heaven... And he sent out arrows and scattered them... He rescued me from my strong enemy, from those who hated me, for they were too mighty for me... he rescued me, because he delighted in me. The LORD dealt with me according to my righteousness... For I have kept the ways of the LORD and have not wickedly departed from my God... I was blameless before him... For you are my lamp, O LORD, and my God lightens my darkness. For by you I can run against a troop, and by my God I can leap over a wall... He trains my hands for war, so that my arms can bend a bow of bronze... I pursued my enemies and destroyed them, and did not turn back until they were consumed... You delivered me from strife with my people; you kept me as the head of the nations; people whom I had not known served me... The LORD lives, and blessed be my rock... For this I will praise you, O LORD, among the nations... Great salvation he brings to his king, and shows steadfast love to his anointed, to David and his offspring forever."

(2 Samuel 22)

28

HOW TO SURVIVE AND THRIVE

(2 Samuel 22)

It was 1783 and the newly created United States was about to unravel. The army was threatening rebellion over unpaid wages and pensions. If payment didn't arrive soon, they promised to start a new nation with General George Washington as king. In that moment, with his and the nation's back against the wall, George Washington had to give the most important speech of his life, and it started with a reminder: "My conduct [up to this point has shown]... you that I have been a faithful friend to the army... I was among the first to embark in the cause... I never left your side for one moment... I have been the constant companion... Of your distress and not among the last to feel and acknowledge your merits... [Why then should you] cast a shade over that glory which [we have]... acquired."[1] In their pain, Washington wanted the army to remember that he was for them, that he was one of them, and that they shouldn't destroy what they had fought for.

We can relate. When our backs are against the wall, it becomes easy to forget what really matters. When we aren't getting what we want and when we want it, we're prone to lose perspective and act foolishly. And that's why it's also crucial for us to remember what God has done. David did this very thing by singing this song. It's a beautiful reminder to us that we too can survive, and even thrive, by looking back with God. So what specifically are we looking for?

Rescue

Our faith is not removed from the real and broken world around us. God really does rescue his people from difficulties and dangers. Western Christians tend to think otherwise. "Sure" we say, "God will save my soul but I'm probably on my own in this life." We tend to put God in one box and the rest of our life in another. David disagrees, "*For the waves of death encompassed me, the torrents of destruction assailed me; the cords of Sheol entangled me; the snares of death confronted me*" (22:5-6). David is describing the battles, enemies, family feuds, national intrigue, and personal sin that surrounded him. "*They were too mighty for me,*" David confesses (22:18). David faced real dangers, and he needed God to provide real rescue.

When a king's story is recorded in history it usually goes one of two ways. Either the king writes it and portrays himself as a hero, or his enemies write it and cast him as a failure. Neither happens here. David speaks on record and recognizes the real hero: *"In my distress I called upon the LORD. . . From his temple he heard my voice. . . The LORD thundered from heaven. . . And he sent out arrows and scattered them. . . He rescued me from my strong enemy, from those who hated me. . ."* (22:7-18). David uses powerful images so that we can not only hear but also feel God's salvation.

Now, to the human observer it didn't always look dramatic when God saved David. That's not what he's claiming. Instead, David is saying that God was personally fighting for him behind the scenes. We need to remember this. Our difficulties and dangers are personal to God. As David learned, this doesn't mean that we can avoid pain, suffering, or death in this life. Rather, it means that God is by our side, providing above and beyond what we need to live out his plans for us.

Blessing

The way we live matters. David reminds us that God rewards faithfulness, "*The Lord dealt with me according to my righteousness; according to the cleanness of my hands he rewarded me... I was blameless before him...*" (22:21–24). Do you have objections to this? I can think of three. First, aren't we saved by grace and not works? Second, how can David claim to be blameless after Bathsheba? Third, even if David was blameless, how can I ever be? Thankfully, these objections misunderstand what David is saying.

Of course the Israelites reading this song would remember Bathsheba-gate. The problem here is us. We tend to use different language and categories than Old Testament believers. We describe people as "saved" or "not saved." They described people as "faithful" or "sinner." The faithful were of course sinful, but they loved God and sought to follow him. The sinners were those who rejected God and his ways. David is saying that though he sinned, he did not belong to the "sinner" category. He belonged to the faithful, the righteous, and the blameless because he loved God and had received forgiveness through repentance. Understanding this, David is reminding us that God blesses our obedience even though it's imperfect. Being saved by grace shouldn't stop us from rejoicing in God's blessing upon obedience.

Power

As we saw with the mighty men, God provides his people with power for life. Listen to the places where God's power shows up for David. *"For by you [God] I can run against a troop, and by my God I can leap over a wall. . . He trains my hands for war, so that my arms can bend a bow of bronze. . ."* (22:30–35). God provides David with power not during a sedate spiritual retreat in the mountains but in the blood, sweat, and tears of his daily life. His God-given work was war and so God was there. It's probably going to look different for us, but the principle remains. God gives what is needed to accomplish his purposes. *"You delivered me from strife with my people; you kept me as the head of the nations; people whom I had not known served me"* (22:44). God provided what was needed to bring the nations close to the true King. He always does.

George Washington's words to the angry army did not receive a positive response. However, before sitting down, he took out a letter to read but stumbled over the words. He put on a pair of glasses. The men had never seen Washington with glasses. "Gentlemen, you must pardon me. I have grown grey in your service and now find myself growing blind."[2] That's when it happened. Something about Washington's weakness and humanity in that moment killed the rebellion. The men, filled with realization and love, began to leave the room, weeping. The United States would survive, and it was because George Washington was just a man, not some eternal hero.

David reminds us of something similar in this song. He was just a man. His enemies were too much for him. He was deeply flawed. But look at what God has done. Look at how he has saved. Look at how he has blessed imperfect obedience. Look at the strength he gave. What a God.

Pause for a Moment

Reflect: When your back is against the wall, what do you tend to forget?

Request: Stop yourself the next time you feel pressure, or anxiety and pray. Ask God to remind you of what he has given you in Christ.

Respond: Start a journal or list in your family of God's help in your everyday life. Read it together as a reminder of his faithfulness.

Now these are the last words of David: The oracle of David, the son of Jesse, the oracle of the man who was raised on high, the anointed of the God of Jacob, the sweet psalmist of Israel: "The Spirit of the LORD speaks by me; his word is on my tongue. The God of Israel has spoken; the Rock of Israel has said to me: When one rules justly over men, ruling in the fear of God, he dawns on them like the morning light, like the sun shining forth on a cloudless morning, like rain that makes grass to sprout from the earth. For does not my house stand so with God? For he has made with me an everlasting covenant, ordered in all things and secure.

For will he not cause to prosper all my help and my desire? But worthless men are all like thorns that are thrown away, for they cannot be taken with the hand; but the man who touches them arms himself with iron and the shaft of a spear, and they are utterly consumed with fire."

(2 Samuel 23:1–7)

29

THE LAST WORDS OF DAVID

(2 Samuel 23:1–7)

Throughout history, the last words of the famous have often been filled with anxiety. Leonardo Da Vinci died anxious about his life's work, "I have offended God and mankind because my work did not reach the quality it should have."[1] The United States President Grover Cleveland died anxiously trying to reassure himself, "I have tried so hard to do right."[2] These men, like so many others, came to the end of their lives with great anxiety.

Are we any different? The older generation often worries about the state of the nation and the faith of their grandchildren. Those in middle age often worry about saving for retirement and having to slow down. Young adults worry about finding a spouse and career. Students worry about surviving school and getting along with parents. All of us manage to find some way to get anxious about the future. In this passage, David has good reason to feel anxiety for his kingdom as he faces death. Nevertheless, he's able to find confidence in God's promises. He's able to say that the future is *ordered* and *secure* in God (23:5). How can God's promises provide us with confidence in the face of real anxiety and stress?

Identity

When God promises us a future hope, he does so while knowing who we are. And as God speaks through David, these last words refer to David as *"the son of Jesse."* God knows where David came from. He's just a man, who comes from a particular tribe, in a small town, from a specific family, with a background in shepherding. Even so, David's identity is not in what he had done for himself or where he came from but in what God has done for him. God *raised* him, God *anointed* him, God *made* him (23:1–5).

The God who anointed this regular man calls himself the *"God of Jacob"* (23:1). Instead of referring to himself as the God of Israel, God is reminding us that he calls and uses regular and broken people like Jacob, the cheater and deceiver of Genesis who later became Israel, and David. Don't think you are excluded from God's future promises because of your ordinary or broken background. All people are ordinary and broken. Likewise, God doesn't make promises because he realizes that one day you'll have it all together. As one wise pastor shares, "The David story is the gospel story, God doing for David what David could never do for himself."[3] God's future promises are not dependent on your future accomplishments but rather God's future work. Your identity is in what God has done and will do for you.

Hope

Not only is our identity secure in God's promises, but so too is the hope of the world. David knew this, *"For does not my house stand so with God? For he has made with me an everlasting covenant, ordered in all things and secure"* (23:5). David's

Kingdom, the hope of the world, was sure in God no matter what else was happening.

Today, we know that the second David, King Jesus, has fulfilled this kingdom in his victory on the cross. Nothing can change the fact that he will return and fully establish this kingdom both in heaven and on earth.[4] And this kingdom is good. *"The God of Israel has spoken... When one rules justly over men, ruling in the fear of God, he dawns on them like the morning light, like the sun shining forth on a cloudless morning, like rain that makes grass to sprout from the earth"* (23:3–4). The kingdom is good because its ruler is.

Specifically, David compares the beauty of the Davidic King to three things all people can appreciate: the comfort of morning's first light, the warmth of the sun in a cloudless sky, and the new life that rain brings. The Kingdom is ruled by one who comforts, refreshes, and gives life, one whom all David's descendants must strive towards and one whom is fully fulfilled in Jesus. Don't lose sight of this. The Good King and Kingdom are here, and the Good King and Kingdom are coming.

Security

God's people regularly rub shoulders with those who do not want the Kingdom or the King. We should pray that they taste the goodness we have received. Some will in time, but some will not. These folks are going down a path that is very different than ours, *"But worthless men are all like thorns that are thrown away, for they cannot be taken with the hand"* (23:6). It's seen as highly inappropriate these days to make distinctions between people. God, however, has no problem doing so. But here's the kicker. This isn't a distinction between good people and bad people. It's a distinction between those who want Jesus and those who don't.

Yes, our God is a missionary God who seeks out the most wicked of men, as should we. But he will also separate those who are his from those who are not. God promises this separation for our good, his glory, and the just destruction of those who have rejected him. *"But the man who touches them [the wicked], arms himself with iron and the shaft of a spear, and they are utterly consumed with fire"* (23:7). God makes war against those who try to choke the life out of the kingdom, and their end is eternal judgment and exclusion. The second David, Jesus, clearly agrees.[5] There is security in the promises of God for all, and only for all, who trust Jesus.

Last words are often important. On his deathbed the great reformer Martin Luther was asked if he stood by all that he had taught about grace and salvation. He affirmed that he did. Then he made it abundantly clear that his hope was not in himself but in another, muttering these last words, "We are all beggars, that is true."[6] Usually being a beggar is not a good thing. But in Jesus' kingdom it's the only option. In fact, it's the only option that opens up God's beautiful kingdom to those who can't earn it but who nevertheless get to enjoy it by grace. When all is said and done, will this be your hope?

Pause for a Moment

Reflect: If you had to write your tombstone or obituary, what would you put? It may sound morbid, but it is good and right to consider what our is our legacy and our hope.

Request: Ask Jesus to give you confidence that his grace is sufficient to cover not only your past sin but also your future sin as well.

Respond: Think of those you know who do not yet know Jesus. How can you begin sharing the hope of the Kingdom with them? It probably needs to start with a loving relationship.

Again the anger of the LORD was kindled against Israel, and he incited David against them, saying, "Go, number Israel and Judah." So the king said to Joab... "Go... and number the people..." But Joab said... "May the LORD... add to the people a hundred times as many as they are... but why does... the king delight in this thing?" But the king's word prevailed... And Joab gave the sum of the numbering... to the king: in Israel there were 800,000... men... and the men of Judah were 500,000. But David's heart struck him... And David said to the LORD, "I have sinned greatly... But now, O LORD, please take away the iniquity of your servant"... The word of the LORD came to the prophet Gad... saying, "Shall three years of famine come to you... Or will you flee three months before your foes... Or shall there be three days' pestilence"... Then David said..."I am in great distress. Let us fall into the hand of the LORD, for his mercy is great; but let me not fall into the hand of man." So the LORD sent a pestilence... And there died...70,000 men. And when the angel stretched out his hand toward Jerusalem to destroy it, the LORD relented... and said... "It is enough..." the angel... was by the threshing floor of Araunah... Then David... said, "Behold, I have sinned... But these sheep, what have they done? Please let your hand be against me and against my father's house." And Gad... said... "raise an altar to the LORD on the threshing floor of Araunah"... And Araunah said, "Why has... the king come...?" David said, "To buy the threshing floor..." Then Araunah said... "All this... Araunah gives to the king."... But the king said... "No... I will buy it... I will not offer burnt offerings to the LORD... that cost me nothing."... David built there an altar to the LORD and offered... offerings. So the LORD responded to the plea... and the plague was averted...

(2 Samuel 24)

WRATH AND MERCY

(2 Samuel 24)

Have you ever made a big mistake only to later realize that it was far worse than you thought? My fourth-grade self saw little harm in turning the living room into a soccer arena until I took a bad shot, watched it fly over the fireplace, strike a giant framed picture, and send glass shattering down upon my youngest brother. In my stunned silence the phone rang. My sister said the words I feared, "It's Mom. She wants you." Only then did I realize how desperate I was for mercy.

Sadly, it often takes moments like this, and worse, to remind us of our need for mercy. Most people function on the assumption that we're basically good. Only when we really mess up is that allusion swept away. Then we begin to see how broken and needy we actually are. Thankfully, God is "merciful and gracious, slow to anger, abounding in steadfast love and faithfulness."[1] So how does God's mercy intersect with our need?

Mercy in Conviction

I wish this were simply a case of Déjà-Vu. Haven't we *already* talked about conviction? Yes, but it wasn't enough. The story starts like this: *"The anger of the LORD was kindled against Israel, and he incited David against them saying, 'Go, number Israel and Judah' "* (24:1). This verse brings up all sorts of questions. Why was God angry with Israel? We're not told, but the safe assumption is always sin. Next, did God really cause David to sin? The Bible tells us that we're always responsible for our sin, so we know that David did what he wanted to do.[2] But was God involved? Again, the Bible tells us that God does no evil, but he does use evil to accomplish his good purposes (think of the cross), and this can go over our understanding pretty quickly.[3] Finally, why was taking a census wrong? The story doesn't tell us, but we can assume that some combination of pride, fear, and selfishness was involved. Even Joab knew it was a bad idea, which is saying something. Bottom line, David and Israel were sinful, and they needed mercy.

Mercy came. *"But David's heart struck him... And David said... 'I have sinned greatly in what I have done. But now, O LORD, please take away the iniquity of your servant' "* (24:10). Compared to David's sin with Bathsheba, we see growth and grace here as David responds quickly to conviction with a prayer of confession and repentance. What a mercy conviction is.

Mercy in Consequences

As the story continues, God forgives David, but he still must face the consequences of his actions. While we'd rather not deal with consequences, David's story reminds us that they are a necessary and just result of sin that will be used by God for our growth.

This is the message David is given: *"Three things I offer you. Choose one of them, that I may do it to you. . . Shall three years of famine come. . . Or will you flee three months before your foes. . . Or shall there be three days pestilence in your land?"* (24:11–13). Can you imagine the dilemma? Thankfully, David knows the one thing he can count on, *"I am in great distress. Let us fall into the hand of the LORD, for his mercy is great; but let me not fall into the hand of man"* (24:14). Looking back on his life, David knows that people are unpredictable. Why would he trust the mercy of enemies, in the case of war, or the mercy of neighboring nations, in the case of a three-month food shortage? David knows that even in wrath, God's mercy can be trusted. David's decision to trust God leaves only the final option: three days of plague. It's worse than we might imagine, 70,000 die. But there is mercy, God stops the plague before Jerusalem is destroyed. Even God's wrath is wrapped in mercy.[4]

Mercy in Restoration

Having faced the consequences, David seeks restoration with God by offering what is basically a self-sacrifice. *"Behold, I have sinned, and I have done wickedly. But these sheep, what have they done? Please let your hand be against me and against my father's house"* (24:17). David's knowledge is limited. Israel is guilty, and there is no way he could ever pay the price personally. Still, this is a beautiful picture of David finally learning what it means to be a Covenant King, to care for the sheep of Israel like the sheep of his father's flock. He's learning.

God in his mercy points David towards a different sacrifice, one with animals. David is offered free cattle for the sacrifice but knows that it must be costly, *"No, but I will buy if from you for a price. I will not offer burnt offerings to the LORD my God that cost me nothing"* (24:24). Though it's harder, David trusts God's path for restoration, a costly sacrifice on the altar, so that David, the people, and the land can be restored from sin.

I remember picking up the phone, hand trembling, as I looked at the soccer ball, shattered picture, and scared little brother. Before my mom could say a word, I confessed everything. The funny thing is, my mom had no idea what had happened, she was simply calling to see what I wanted for lunch. I remember telling her that I didn't deserve lunch. I was right. Nevertheless, my mom came home with lunch. Of course, it's illegal to starve your children, but she could have made me eat celery. Instead, she picked up something tasty. I've long since forgotten whatever consequences came later that day, all I remember was this small act of undeserved mercy.

This book closes with David and Israel once again finding themselves in a huge mess. And yet, once again, through his mercy and grace, God restores them. Isn't this the heart of the whole David story? That while imperfect, David learns where to find mercy for his sin and the sins of his people. Hundreds of years later, about five miles from the altar in this story, a baby was born. The first verse of the New Testament tells us that this Jesus was the son of David. It was just a short walk from this same altar to where this God-man Jesus would put on a cross, as the divine Priest-King of Israel, so that he could make a costly sacrifice for us, in which he exchanged the wrath of God for the mercy of God, so that we could be freely received in grace. You need both mercy and grace. And God, in his fierce love, has given them both to you forever in the Second David.

Pause for a Moment

Reflect: Were you surprised by how messy, broken, and rough David's story was?

Request: Ask God to show you the presence and work of his mercy and grace in your life.

Respond: Live with bold confidence today, not in yourself, but in the one who has given you grace.

If this book has left you interested in more study on the life of King David or the biblical books that *Fierce Grace* was based upon (1 and 2 Samuel), I encourage you to first consider Dale Ralph Davis' incredible commentaries on 1 and 2 Samuel in the Focus On The Bible Commentary Series. In my eyes, the greatest fault of *Fierce Grace* is that it relies too heavily on Davis' work. His commentaries are easily accessible, filled with wonderful illustration and application, and provide hearty biblical insight. Davis' works are just a small step up from *Fierce Grace* in terms of reading difficulty, and I'd likewise recommend his works on the Psalms. I love the Word of God more deeply every time I read from Davis.

Another accessible resource is Eugene Peterson's *Leap Over A Wall.* This book does a great job of helping the reader feel the story and setting of David's life but wanders from the biblical text at times, mainly in innocent ways. Likewise, Joyce Baldwin's short commentary on 1 and 2 Samuel in the Tyndale Old Testament Commentary Series is a great place to start but is very limited due to its size. Mark Boda's *After God's Own Heart: The Gospel According To David* is a fairly easy-to-read topical resource that explores the most important themes of David's life in a short amount of space. In terms of historical fiction, I commend Cliff Graham's creative and gritty *Lion of War* series.

Finally, more comprehensive resources to consult include David Firth's commentary in the Apollos Old Testament Commentary Series and David Tsumura's 1st Samuel commentary in the New International Commentary on the Old Testament Series. While Firth's commentary is quite readable, Tsumura's is highly technical and should only be consulted by those well versed in Hebrew. May Christ bless your future studies in his Word!

STEPHEN R. MOREFIELD (M.Div., Covenant Theological Seminary) pastors Christ Covenant Evangelical Presbyterian Church in the wonderful small town of Leoti, KS. Stephen and his wife, Morgan, have two children. Stephen has also ministered, in various capacities, in suburban Kansas City, urban St. Louis, and rural Iowa. He currently chairs the Care of Candidates Committee of the Presbytery of the West (EPC) and the Wichita County Ministerial Alliance. He is originally from Kansas City, holding tight to his love of the Chiefs, Royals, Jayhawks, Sporting, and, of course, good barbecue.

Chapter 1

[1] Proverbs 9:10.

[2] These events are covered in the biblical books of Genesis through Judges.

[3] Genesis 17:6; Genesis 49:10; Deuteronomy 17:14–20; and Deuteronomy 18:15.

[4] Psalm 93.

[5] Revelation 21.

Chapter 2

[1] Terry Crowdy, *Deceiving Hitler* (Oxford: Osprey Publishing, 2013), 195.

[2] 1 Chronicles 28:9.

[3] 1 Samuel 9-15.

Chapter 3

[1] You are very welcome Rees Wedel.

[2] Colossians 1:13.

[3] Dale Ralph Davis, *1 Samuel* (Great Britain: Christian Focus Publishers Ltd., 2000), 184.

[4] Eugene Peterson, *Leap Over A Wall* (New York, NY: Harper Collins, 1998), 40.

[5] Saul was Israel's covenant head. While it may have been permissible for another warrior to represent Israel in battle, especially in the case of an elderly king, it was ultimately Saul's responsibility. Someone had to fight Goliath and the buck was supposed to stop with Saul.

[6] Davis, *1 Samuel,* 179.

Chapter 4

[1] Matthew 28:20.

[2] For the idea of "country music," see Davis, *1 Samuel, 193.*

[3] Davis, *1 Samuel*, 196.

[4] Ibid.

[5] Matthew 27:46.

[6] Old Testament believers were saved the same way Christians are today: through faith in God's provision of grace. Although they didn't yet see Jesus' sacrifice as clearly as we do, God applies that grace to them through their faith, which of course is a gift from Him as well.

Chapter 5

[1] Chris Ballard, *Jump He Said. And They Fell,* Reader's Digest. June 1, 2015.

[2] Davis, *1 Samuel*, 212.

[3] Jill Reilly, "Police Officer Saves The Life Of A Suicidal Woman By Handcuffing Himself To Her And Throwing Away The Key." *Daily Mail.* August 16th, 2013. Accessed October 9th, 2017. http://www.dailymail.co.uk/news/article-2395551/Beijing-Chinese-police-officer-saves-life-suicidal-woman-handcuffing-her.html.

Chapter 6

[1] Romans 8:28.

[2] The Book of Ruth.

[3] 2 Peter 1:19.

Chapter 7

[1] Mike Holmes, "What Would Happen If The Church Tithed?" *Relevant Magazine.* March 8, 2016. Accessed October 9, 2017. https://relevantmagazine.com/god/church/what-would-happen-if-church-tithed

[2] Ed Stetzer, "New Research: Less Than 20% of Churchgoers Read The Bible Daily." *Christianity Today.* September 13, 2012. Accessed October 9, 2017. http://www.christianitytoday.com/edstetzer/2012/september/new-research-less-than-20-of-churchgoers-read-bible-daily.html

[3] Jon D. Wilke, "Churchgoers Believe In Sharing Faith, Most Never Do." *Lifeway.* Undated. Accessed October 9, 2017. http://www.lifeway.com/Article/research-survey-sharing-christ-2012

4 Proverbs 3:5.

5 Jeremiah 10:23 and 1 Samuel 16:12.

6 Romans 12:19.

7 Revelation 19.

Chapter 8

1 Scripture condemns polygamy (1 Timothy 3:2). Even in the passages where it is practiced the results always serve as a warning. That being said, David's marriage to Abigail comes at a time where his first wife has been taken from him (25:44). Sadly, David continued to add wives, as verse 43 makes clear. David's son Solomon will follow in this sin and pay the ultimate price for his polygamy in 1 Kings 11:4.

Chapter 9

1 Proverbs 14:12.

2 The core insight of this paragraph comes from Dale Ralph Davis. Davis, *1 Samuel*, 286–287.

Chapter 10

1 John 5.

2 Philippians 1:6.

3 1 Kings 19.

4 Ezra 1.

5 Matthew 13.

6 1 Samuel 23.

7 Matthew 26: 24 and 1 Peter 2:23–24.

8 Romans 9:16.

9 Ephesians 2:8–9.

Chapter 11

1 2 Corinthians 3:5.

2 *Taken*, Directed by Pierre Morel, France: EuropaCorp, 2008.

3 1 Samuel 22.

4 The ephod was a, "Priestly garment connected with seeking a word from God... the ephod was associated with the presence of God or those who had a

special relationship with God. It is portrayed as a special source of divine guidance." Daniel B. McGee, *Holman Illustrated Bible Dictionary,* "Ephod." Nashville, Holman Bible Publishers, 2003.

[5] Matthew 11:28.

[6] Matthew 20:15.

Chapter 13

[1]Frank W. Abagnale & Stan Redding, *Catch Me If You Can: The True Story of A Real Fake* (New York: Broadway Books, 2000).

[2] 1 Samuel 16.

[3] Genesis 49.

[4] Genesis 17.

[5] While God chose Saul to rule previously, God made it clear that Saul was the king the "people" wanted. Yes, Saul was part of God's ultimate plan but no, Saul was not the King that God would use to start an eternal dynasty leading to the Chosen One, Jesus Christ. David, on the other hand, is the man that God has chosen for this purpose.

[6] Linda Langelo, "Plant Native Grass To Improve Water Quality" *Journal-Advocate Online.* October 12, 2017. Accessed November 6, 2017. http://www.journal-advocate.com/business/sterling-agriculture/ci_31369568/plant-native-grass-improve-water-quality).

Chapter 14

[1] 2 Samuel 2:14–16.

[2] Men and women created in the image of God are never to be treated or viewed merely as property.

[3] Again, the way that women are treated as political pawns in this story is both tragic and wrong in the Lord's eyes. Men *and* women are equally created in God's image.

[4] Matthew 6:10.

Chapter 15

[1] 1 Samuel 16:7.

[2] Baanah and Rechab are introduced right after it is announced that Saul's son Ish-bosheth has lost his courage and right before it is announced that Saul's son Jonathan has a surviving son who was crippled in an accident.

[3] Dale Ralph Davis, *2 Samuel* (Great Britain: Christian Focus Publishers Ltd., 2001), 50-51.

[4] Ibid., 53.

Chapter 16

[1] Genesis 3:15.

[2] Genesis 17:6.

[3] Deuteronomy 18:15.

[4] David's adding of more wives in this chapter is ample evidence of David's imperfection and sin.

[5] This passage could lead a person to believe that David has a low or disparaging view of the disabled. Quite the opposite is the case, as we'll come to see in David's interactions with Jonathan's only surviving son.

[6] Genesis 15.

[7] Isaiah 65; 66; 2 Peter 3; and Revelation 21.

Chapter 17

[1] 1 Samuel 2.

[2] Psalm 63.

[3] 1 Samuel 4.

[4] Numbers 10:35–36.

[5] Numbers 4:5–6, 15, 18–20.

[6] David Kirby, "Did a Wild Orca Really Attack a Diver In New Zealand?" *TakePart.com* February 24, 2014. Accessed November 27, 2017. http://www.takepart.com/article/2014/02/24/did-wild-orca-really-just-at-tack-diver-new-zealand

[7] *http://www.freemorgan.org/wp-content/uploads/2012/10/list_of_inci-dents.pdf.*

[8] Isaiah 11:3 & Jeremiah 33:9.

Chapter 18

[1] Davis, *2 Samuel,* 88–90.

[2] Ibid., 76-77.

Chapter 19

[1] Which, by the way, wasn't as rosy as we've come to believe. In fact, the Church has always struggled with sin! Check out 1 Corinthians 5 as an example.

[2] While David's process with the Moabites would be unthinkable today and seems unnecessarily harsh, we have to remember that God had patiently endured the Moabites (and their sin) for generations. They not only deserved God's wrath, as all sinners do, but David was also uniquely called to be God's agent of judgment towards them. Therefore, we should really be amazed that any were spared and, more importantly, that we've been spared by Jesus' death on the cross. It is this message that we are called to now spread.

[3] Davis, *2 Samuel,* 112.

[4] Isaiah 56:6–7.

[5] Davis, *2 Samuel,* 115.

Chapter 20

[1] Ephesians 2:1-3 & 8–9.

[2] Leviticus 18:16–23.

[3] Romans 5:8.

[4] Hebrews 4:15.

[5] Davis, *2 Samuel,* 126.

Chapter 21

[1] "Quebec Invention: The World-Famous Ski-Doo Was Named Because Of A Typing Error." *Canada Cool Online* Accessed January 15, 2018.   http://www.canadacool.com/location/quebec-invention-ski-doo/

[2] Nasrine Abushakra, "How Businesses Lose Millions When They Ignore Cultural Sensitivity Training." *Dr. Nasrine Online* December 3, 2015. Accessed January 15, 2018. http://www.drnasrine.com/how-businesses-lose-millions-when-they-ignore-cultural-sensitivity-training/.

[3] John Calvin, *Sermons on 2 Samuel* trans. Douglass Kelly (Edinburgh: Banner of Truth, 1992), 463–69.

Chapter 22

[1] Psalm 19.

2 Job 31:1, Psalm 16, Psalm 63, Psalm 107:9, Deuteronomy 17:15–17, and Exodus 20.

3 2 Samuel 23:39. Uriah, as a foreigner, likely joined David's men during David's time as an outlaw (see 1 Samuel 22). David was clearly the military and spiritual leader of this group and so it's more than likely that Uriah's faith either started under David's discipleship or at the very least grew immensely through it. This makes David's adultery with Bathsheba all the more sickening.

4 Genesis 3:15.

5 Psalm 32.

6 John 10:28.

Chapter 23

1 Hebrews 9:22.

2 The first of Luther's 95 Theses.

Chapter 24

1 Mary Bowerman, "Police: Bank robbers' posts photos of cash on Facebook" *USA Today Network* September 30, 2015. Accessed December 27, 2017. https://www.usatoday.com/story/news/nation-now/2015/09/30/alleged-bank-robbers-posts-photos-cash-facebook-ohio/73075860/

2 From Owen's *The Mortification of Sin in Believers.*

3 These suggestions are adapted from John Piper's strategy for fighting against the particular temptation of lust. The full strategy, which the author highly commends, can be found here: https://www.desiringgod.org/articles/anthem-strategies-for-fighting-lust.

Chapter 25

1 Carol Lea Mueller, *The Quotable John Wayne: The Grit and Wisdom of an American Icon* (Plymouth, UK: Taylor Trade Publishing, 2007) pg. 41.

2 *Parks and Recreation,* "Lil' Sebastian." Episode 16. Directed by Dean Holland. Written by Greg Daniels, Michael Schur, Daniel Goor, Katie Dippold, and Harris Wittels. NBC, May 19, 2011.

3 Dennis Linn, Sheila Fabricant Linn, & Matthew Linn, *Sleeping With Bread* *(Mexico: Paulist Press, 1995), 1.*

Chapter 26

[1] New Living Translation.

[2] Isaiah 55:9.

[3] Willa Cather, *Death Comes for The Archbishop* (Vintage Classics: New York, 1990), 189–192.

[4] Luke 22:42.

Chapter 27

[1] Sean Astin, *Return of the King. DVD.* Directed by Peter Jackson. USA: New Line Cinema, 2003.

[2] David G Firth., *1 & 2 Samuel* (Nottingham: Apollos, 2009), 511.

[3] This is different than choosing to live as a lone ranger for it is a temporary stand taken out of necessity, not choice.

Chapter 28

[1] Eric Metaxas, *Seven Men* (Thomas Nelson: Nashville, 2013), 20–21.

[2] Ibid., 23.

Chapter 29

[1] John J. Barber, *My Almost for His Highest* (Eugene, OR: Wipf & Stock, 2010), 116.

[2] Paul F. Boller, *Presidential Anecdotes* (New York: Oxford Press, 1996), 181.

[3] Peterson, *Leap Over A Wall*, 211.

[4] Revelation 21.

[5] Contrary to popular opinion, Jesus talked about judgment a lot. For example, Matthew 25:41–46 or Mark 9:42–50.

[6] R.C. Sproul & Stephen Nichols, editors, *The Legacy of Luther* (Orlando, FL; Reformation Trust, 2016), 74.

Chapter 30

[1] Exodus 34:6.

[2] Romans 14:12 and James 1:13.

[3] Romans 8:28.

[4] Galatians 3:13 and Davis, *2 Samuel,* 3:20.